The West Country

The West Country

Text by Robin Whiteman

Photographs by Rob Talbot

Weidenfeld and Nicolson
London

Text and photographs © Talbot-Whiteman 1993

The right of Robin Whiteman and Rob Talbot to be identified as
authors of this work has been asserted by them in accordance with
the Copyright, Designs and Patents Act 1988.

First published in Great Britain in 1993 by George Weidenfeld and
Nicolson Ltd, Orion House, 5 Upper St Martin's Lane, London WC2H 9EA

Designed by Joy FitzSimmons
Map by Bob Monks

British Library Cataloguing-in-Publication Data
A catalogue record for this book is available from the British Library.

ISBN 0–297–83158–5

Typeset by Deltatype Limited, Ellesmere Port
Printed and bound in Italy

Endpapers: Gurnard's Head, Cornwall
Half-title page: Polpeor Cove, Cornwall
Title page: Polperro, Cornwall

Contents

Acknowledgements   6

Author's Note   6

Map of the West Country   7

INTRODUCTION   8

LAND'S END AND SOUTH-WESTERN CORNWALL   12

TRURO AND CENTRAL CORNWALL   32

TINTAGEL AND NORTH-EASTERN CORNWALL   54

PLYMOUTH AND SOUTH-WESTERN DEVON   76

LYDFORD AND DARTMOOR   92

EXETER AND SOUTH-EASTERN DEVON   114

ILFRACOMBE AND NORTHERN DEVON   128

TAUNTON AND EXMOOR   136

Photographer's Notes   155

Selected Properties and Regional Offices   156

Select Bibliography   158

Index   159

Acknowledgements

Robin Whiteman and Rob Talbot would particularly like to acknowledge the generous co-operation of English Heritage (Properties in Care – South-West) and the three National Trust Regional Offices of Cornwall, Devon and Wessex for allowing them to take photographs of their properties and sites featured in this book. They are also extremely grateful to: Philip Jackson, Theatre Manager, The Minack Theatre; Canonteign Falls and Country Park; Barry Litton, Hermitage, St Nectan's Glen; Joanne Hillman, Librarian, Cornish Studies Library, Redruth (Cornish County Council); Elisabeth A. Stuart, Archivist, Duchy of Cornwall; Daisy Blackmore, Warden at Gwennap Pit, Busveal. Special thanks go to Judith Dooling. Appreciation goes also to all those individuals and organizations too numerous to mention by name who nevertheless have made a valuable contribution. Deserving a special acknowledgement are Michael Dover and Colin Grant at Weidenfeld and Nicolson.

Author's Note

The West Country, for the purposes of this book, covers both Devon and Cornwall, including the two National Parks of Dartmoor and Exmoor, Bodmin Moor and the Land's End peninsula, as well as that part of Somerset, west of Barnstaple and Taunton, which embraces the Quantock Hills. Cornwall has been divided into three parts (based largely on the local government districts created in 1974): north-eastern Cornwall, central Cornwall and south-western Cornwall. Devon has been divided into four sections: northern Devon (north of Okehampton and west of the River Exe, but excluding Exmoor); eastern Devon (south and east of the Dartmoor National Park and the rivers Exe and Teign, including the coast from Teignmouth to the Dorset border); Dartmoor (the National Park and its western extension to the Cornish border); and south-western Devon (from Plymouth and the Tamar to the River Teign). Exmoor has been included in the west Somerset section.

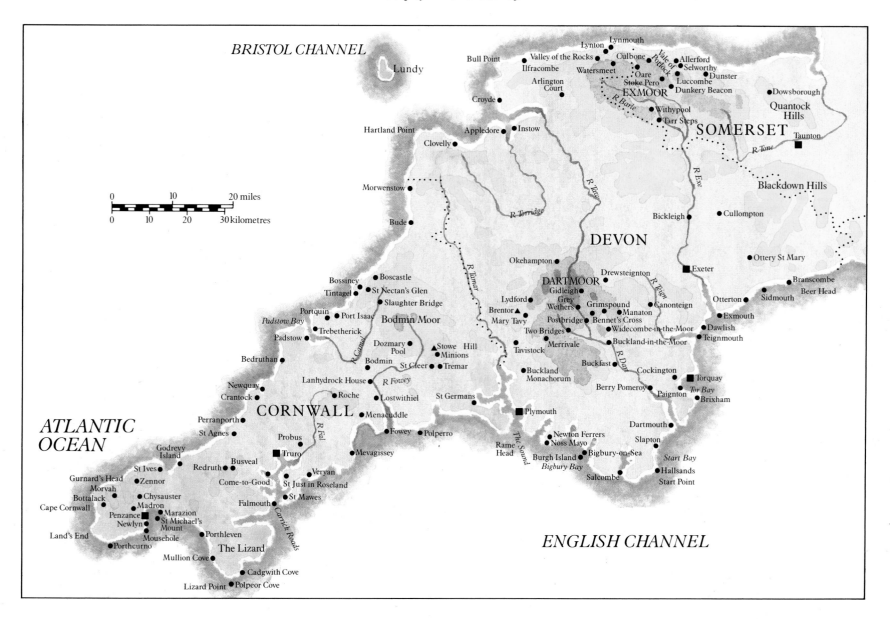

Introduction

BOWERMAN'S NOSE
Manaton

Rising from Hayne Down on Dartmoor, less than a mile south-west of the village of Manaton, is a prominent thirty-foot stack of fissured granite known as Bowerman's Nose. Over thousands of years the rock has cracked and weathered into a formation with an almost human profile. Nicholas Toms Carrington described the natural rock pile in *Dartmoor: A Descriptive Poem* (1826), 'On the very edge / Of the vast moorland, startling every eye / A shape enormous rises! High it towers / Above the hill's bold brow, and seen from far, / Assumes the human form; a granite god – / To whom, in days long flown, the suppliant knee / In trembling homage bow'd. The hamlets near, / Have legends rude connected with the spot / (Wild swept by every wind), on which he stands / The giant of the moor.' Despite the fact that 'Bowerman' is thought by some to be derived from the Celtic *vawr-maen* meaning 'great stone', local legend persists that he was a Norman bowman or archer. A great hunter, he and his hounds were turned to stone either for disturbing a coven of witches or for persisting in hunting on a Sunday.

S ince long before, and for long after, the year AD 495 – when a vision of St Michael appeared to Cornish fishermen on the island rock of St Michael's Mount – the wonders of the West Country have held an irresistible appeal. England's wild and mysterious south-west peninsula – or 'West-of-Wessex', as Hardy termed the region – with its rich Celtic heritage, stands uniquely apart from the rest of England, almost as if it were a foreign land. Indeed, as Tristram Risdon wrote *c.* 1620, it was 'anciently one province, one nation, and one kingdom'. As the land narrows the sky widens, and the sea – which is never far away – increasingly makes its powerful presence felt, until finally at Land's End – the beginning and the end – the pounding Atlantic spray turns the grey granite cliffs almost white.

John Taylor, the 'Water Poet', made the long journey to Land's End from London in 1649, the year Charles I was executed. A Royalist with a lame leg, embittered by defeat, 'having travelled North, and South, and East', he meant to end his 'travels with the West'. '*Cornwall* is the *Cornucopia*,' he wrote, 'the complete and replete horn of abundance for high churlish hills, and affable courteous people.' Comprising Devon, Cornwall and west Somerset, and bounded in the north by the Bristol Channel, in the west by the Atlantic Ocean and in the south by the English Channel, the West Country is a land of breathtaking scenery with over 500 miles of spectacular coastline and two National Parks, Dartmoor and Exmoor, created in 1951 and 1954 respectively.

Dartmoor, covering an area of 365 square miles, is a high moorland mass of granite, crowned by grey, shattered tors, weathered into weird and grotesque shapes, all uniquely different. By way of contrast, Exmoor, 265 square miles in area, is an undulating upland plateau of green, hedged pastures and heather- and bracken-clad moorland, gouged by deep, wooded valleys. Largely composed of soft Devonian slates and sandstones, the plateau rises to the single conical peak of Dunkery Beacon (1704 ft). To the north it ends in high, rounded cliffs, reaching over 1000 feet in places, before dipping headlong down to the sea. The coastal viewpoints from the top are the highest in England.

There are two main theories for the formation of the tors: one says that the granite chemically rotted in a warm humid climate; the other suggests that the rock disintegrated in more recent periglacial (arctic) conditions. Both agree, however, that the amount of weathering and the final shape of the tors were controlled by the jointing – the widely spaced vertical and horizontal cracks that divide the granite into large blocks. The joints were formed millions of years ago as the original, molten granite magma solidified, and also as the weight of the overlying rocks, gradually removed by erosion, released the pressure on the granite beneath. The tors were finally revealed during the Ice Ages as the less resistant material (growan) was carried downhill by solifluction, a process by which the granite blocks, together with a mass of debris, slid down and over a permanently frozen incline. The granite blocks found scattered on the slopes below the tors are known as clitter or, when used as a building material, moorstone. Sometimes granite slabs weighing many tons may be so precariously balanced that they will rock or pivot when subjected to a small amount of pressure. These are called 'logan stones' and are found in both Devon and Cornwall. Granite appears in many forms and colours. On Dartmoor alone some 400 different types have been identified.

The mineral wealth of the West Country has been exploited for centuries. Stone was used by prehistoric people to build houses, walls and ritual monuments. Tin and copper were worked by Bronze Age communities to make tools and weapons. Limestone has been dug for mortar since Roman times and, later, for agricultural purposes. Slate has been quarried for roofing tiles and gravestones, while china and ball clay have been mined since the early nineteenth century.

Scattered throughout the region are haunting reminders of the distant and not-so-distant past: chambered tombs, mysterious *fogous* (underground passages), sacred wells, buried chapels, deserted villages, castle ruins, huers' huts (fishermen's lookouts), abandoned engine houses and granite tram-rails. But the West Country is much more than its scenery, much more than its wealth of archaeological, historical and industrial sites; it is a land renowned for the character, life and traditions of its people. This is the legendary realm of King Arthur; the whispered haunt of smugglers and privateers; the secret abode of giants, mermaids and piskies; the source of inspiration for countless artists and writers; the magnet for missionary saints from Brittany, Ireland and Wales; the offshore graveyard for over a thousand ships. There is a strange magic and mystery in this once remote corner of England. It beckons us still.

CHYSAUSTER ANCIENT VILLAGE

Three miles north of Penzance, in the parish of Gulval, lies the ancient village of Chysauster, inhabited in the late Iron Age and Roman times. It was rediscovered in 1849 and first excavated in 1873 by William Copeland Borlase. It stands on the western slopes of a hill topped by the earthwork remains of an Iron Age hillfort, Castle-an-Dinas. Today, much of the surrounding moorland – with its extensive prehistoric field systems – is agricultural land. The settlement consists of nine large oval houses, eight of which are arranged in pairs on either side of a street. The rooms of each house, originally roofed with turf or thatch, are grouped around an open central courtyard. South of the main village are the remains of a *fogou*, an underground passage, which may once have been within a much larger settlement. Dry-stone walled and roofed over with stone slabs, the passage was covered with earth and may have been used to store food. Better preserved examples can be seen at Carn Euny Iron Age settlement, near Sancreed, and Halliggye, near Helston. Like the village, both are in the care of English Heritage.

Land's End and South-Western Cornwall

LANYON QUOIT
Madron

Midway between Madron and Trevowhan, a few yards north of the road, stands Lanyon Quoit, a Neolithic chamber tomb possibly dating from 2000 BC. The stones originally stood at the northern end of an earthen burial mound, approximately ninety feet long by forty feet wide. The seventeen-foot-long capstone rests on three five-foot-high supports. Before the twenty-ton capstone was dislodged in a storm in 1815, it stood about eight feet from the ground on four upright supports. It was re-erected on three supports in 1824. The stones at the southern end of the quoit are thought to be the remains of a smaller burial chamber or cist. Chun Quoit, two miles to the west, stands near Chun Castle. Resembling an enormous mushroom, the Neolithic tomb, with one closed chamber, was originally covered by a round barrow about thirty-five feet in diameter. The ruined pumping engine house on the horizon marks the site of the old Ding Dong mine, one of the oldest tin mines in Cornwall, reputed to have been worked in pre-Christian times.

One of the greatest concentrations of prehistoric sites in Britain occurs on the wild, grey granite peninsula of Land's End. Known to Classical writers as 'Belerion', the eighty-seven-square-mile upland mass is separated from the rest of Cornwall by a low-lying isthmus four miles wide, partly formed by the valleys of the rivers Red and Hayle. Most of the area has been officially designated an Area of Outstanding Natural Beauty and is known to have contained at least 1200 ancient sites, 800 of which can still be seen. Archaeological records put the figure for the whole of Cornwall at around 40,000. But, despite the wealth of prehistoric remains scattered throughout the county, none can compare in age to the relics found across the border in Kent's Cavern, Torquay.

In 1989, using the latest scientific techniques, experts established that the cavern was the oldest identified human settlement in Britain, dating back at least 500,000 years. Between 1865 and 1880 excavation of the horizontal cave system, covering three acres, yielded some 80,000 different prehistoric objects, including the bones of mammoths, sabre-toothed tigers, reindeers and bears. A jawbone discovered in the cavern in 1927 was found by radio-carbon dating to be 31,000 years old, making it the oldest specimen of *Homo sapiens sapiens* – or completely modern man – to be found anywhere in Europe. (It is worth noting that fragments of the skull of a specimen of *Homo sapiens*, thought to date from about 230,000 BC, were discovered in 1935–6 near Swanscombe, Kent.)

Over the past two million years Britain has experienced a series of Ice Ages, the last ending in about 8000 BC. Yet the ice sheet never engulfed Devon and Cornwall, although it came close to doing so about 270,000 years ago, when the Bristol Channel and the northern parts of the Isles of Scilly were affected. The close proximity of the ice brought freezing arctic conditions to the region, similar to those experienced today in Siberia.

As the ice melted, large areas of low-lying land that had previously been above the sea were gradually swallowed by the waves. Perhaps the legendary lost land of Lyonesse, the British Atlantis, is a distant memory of this post-glacial drowning of the landscape. A milder and wetter climate encouraged the rapid spread of vegetation and in a relatively short while the whole country, apart from a few upland areas, was covered with a vast forest of mainly deciduous trees. Low-lying parts of this ancient forest – where trees grew close to the former shoreline – were submerged. There are around thirty submerged forest sites in

Cornwall, some of which may be revealed at exceptionally low tides. These include Mount's Bay, Pendower Beach, Maenporth and Daymer Bay.

The earliest people to inhabit the forests of the West Country were nomadic hunters, food gatherers and fishermen who came to Britain when it was part of the land mass of Europe (it finally became an island in about 5000 BC). The improved climate encouraged further waves of immigrants: Mesolithic groups of hunters and non-permanent or seasonal settlers who established their territorial hunting grounds on various upland sites throughout the region. Their impact on the landscape was minimal, but evidence of their presence (mainly in the form of flint tools) has been found in a number of places, including Dartmoor, Bodmin Moor and the Land's End peninsula.

The process of forest clearance, begun by the Mesolithic hunters, was accelerated by the Neolithic (New Stone Age) people, who came from mainland Europe in about 3500 BC, the earliest groups possibly arriving in the West Country as early as *c.* 4000 BC. They were the first to found permanent settlements, cultivating the soil to grow crops to feed themselves and their livestock. Excavations at Carn Brea, near Redruth, have revealed a Neolithic settlement dating back to 3900 BC, making it one of the oldest in Britain. These early farmers buried their dead in long barrows, rare in Cornwall. More typical of the region are the great chamber tombs, known locally as 'quoits', consisting of a stone burial chamber topped by a huge capstone and originally covered by soil. A later wave of Neolithic megalith builders created a variation of these 'Penwith chamber tombs', with an entrance leading directly into a narrow, rectangular stone chamber roofed with flat slabs. Found mainly in the Isles of Scilly, with several on Land's End, they are known as 'Scillonian chamber tombs' or 'entrance graves'.

From about 2500 BC the Beaker people, thought to have originated in the Rhine basin, settled in Britain and began to construct round barrows, stone circles, menhirs (standing stones) and stone rows – which continued to be built throughout much of the Bronze Age. Named after the beaker-shaped pots found in their graves, they brought with them a knowledge of metal-working, and soon began to exploit the plentiful supplies of copper and tin found in Cornwall and Devon. By about 1900 BC the technique of making bronze, an alloy of copper and tin, had been discovered, possibly in the Land's End peninsula where the metals occur naturally together. A further wave of settlers, joining forces with the Beaker people and creating the Early Bronze Age Wessex Culture, built up a lucrative West Country trade in exporting the smelted ores to Brittany and the Mediterranean.

The people of the Middle Bronze Age, who arrived *c.* 1500 BC, farmed large areas of Dartmoor and Bodmin Moor. Evidence of their occupation – hut circles, field systems and 'reaves' (linear stone banks used to mark boundaries) – still survive. They were followed *c.* 500 BC by Iron Age traders and settlers, who built numerous hillforts and cliff castles as well as the ancient villages of Chysauster and Porthmeor. Known as Celts, these people are mentioned by the Greek historian Diodorus Siculus, who quotes from the lost annals of Pytheas, a Greek geographer from Marseilles writing *c.* 325 BC:

> The inhabitants of that part of Britain called Belerion are friendly to strangers and, from their contact with foreign merchants, are civilized in their way of life. They work the ground from which they extract tin. It is rocky but contains earthy veins, the produce of which they grind down, smelt and purify. The metal is then beaten into ingots shaped like astragali [knuckle bones] and carried to a certain island lying off the coast which is called Ictis [thought to be St Michael's Mount]. During the ebb of the tide, the intervening space is left dry and they carry the tin, in great quantities, over to the island in their wagons. Here then the merchants buy the tin from the natives and carry it over to Gaul and, after travelling overland for about thirty days, they finally bring their loads on horses to the mouth of the Rhone.

Although the Romans and the Anglo-Saxons penetrated as far west as Cornwall, their impact on the inhabitants of the south-west peninsula was relatively small. The language spoken by the Celts was the native tongue of the Cornish people until it finally disappeared in the seventeenth and eighteenth centuries. As A. K. Hamilton Jenkin said in his preface to *Cornwall and its People*: 'It is not without reason that the Cornish people have always been regarded as a race apart. Even today, despite the loss of their native language, they retain, to a surprising degree, the characteristics which mark them still as Celts.'

GODREVY LIGHTHOUSE
St Ives Bay

Standing on an island in St Ives Bay, Godrevy Lighthouse was erected in 1858 and was in operation the following year. The tower is eighty-six feet high, octagonal in shape and painted white. It was built to warn vessels of the Stones, a dangerous reef which extends out to sea from the island for a mile-and-a-half. Numerous ships have been wrecked on the reef and island, including the passenger steamer *Nile* in 1854, which led to the establishment by Trinity House of the navigational light (but not before a further two ships had foundered on the rocks). Virginia Woolf, who holidayed as a child at St Ives, is thought to have been inspired by Godrevy when she wrote *To The Lighthouse* (1927). Today the lighthouse is unmanned, but the remains of the keeper's cottage can clearly be seen. A strong lightweight chair, suspended by a taut wire rope, carried the keepers across the narrow channel between the mainland and the island. It was probably dismantled in the 1920s when motor boats were introduced. Buried beneath the nearby towans or dunes, is St Gothian's (or Gwithian's) chapel or oratory, dating from the seventh or eighth century. It was discovered in 1827 but is now covered again by sand.

ST IVES

The ancient market town and port of St Ives was the principal pilchard fishery in Cornwall, exporting fish to the Mediterranean, until the end of the nineteenth century. It also exported copper and tin. Today the harbour is mainly used by pleasure craft. Smeaton's Pier was built in 1767–70 and lengthened in 1888–90. The shorter West Pier was constructed in 1894 as a loading jetty for locally quarried roadstone. The old fishing quarter is noted for its granite cottages, narrow alleys and cobbled streets. The miners lived higher up the slope in 'Stennack', which it was usual to refer to as 'Up-along', while the lower area around the harbour would be called 'Down-along'. St Ives is named after St Ia, who built an oratory here in the fifth century, possibly on the site of the present parish church, which dates from the early fifteenth century. The buttressed and pinnacled granite tower was constructed of huge granite stones brought by boat from Zennor. The arrival of the railway in 1877 led to the town's development into a popular holiday resort. St Ives also attracted many artists, including Bernard Leach (1887–1979) and Barbara Hepworth (1903–75), whose home and studio is now a museum.

ZENNOR

The tiny village of Zennor, some four miles south-west of St Ives, nestles in a sheltered valley leading down to the Atlantic. A former agricultural, fishing and tin-mining settlement, Zennor is dominated by its granite church, dedicated to St Senara. Dating from the twelfth century, the church is thought to stand on the site of a small Celtic chapel. Carved on a bench end inside is a mermaid holding a mirror and comb; she is said to have been so captivated by the voice of a chorister, Mathey or Matthew Trewhella, that she lured him away forever into the sea at Pendour Cove. A memorial to John Davey (1812–91) states that he 'was the last to possess any considerable traditional knowledge of the Cornish language'. D. H. Lawrence stayed in the Tinners Arms in 1916. The Wayside Museum depicts life in the 'churchtown' from prehistoric times. Zennor Quoit, the remains of a Neolithic round barrow, stands on Zennor Hill, about a mile east of the village. The tomb contains two chambers which were once capped by an enormous stone, eighteen feet long and nine feet wide, now dislodged. Excavations have found bones, flints, pottery and a perforated whetstone.

TREGERTHEN AND TREMEDDA
Zennor

'Can you imagine the excitement which a line gives you when you draw it across a surface? It is like walking through the country from St Ives to Zennor' (Ben Nicholson 1894–1982). There are a number of alternative footpaths between St Ives and Zennor. The South-West Coast Path is one; another passes just inland, through the hamlets and farms of Hellesveor, Trowan, Trevalgan, Trevega, Wicca, Tregerthen and Tremedda. The granite moorland is essentially rough and wild; strewn with enormous boulders and covered with bracken and gorse, it is inhabited by a wealth of flora and fauna. In part the land has been cultivated, and its pattern of small, irregular fields enclosed by huge granite boulders is based on much earlier prehistoric farms. Today farmers are encouraged by grants to work the land traditionally, including maintaining the small field patterns and grazing rough land with cattle. D. H. Lawrence rented the cottage known as Higher Tregerthen in 1916, staying there with his German wife Frieda. Part of *Women in Love* was written there. The following year he was suspected of spying for the Germans and was ordered to leave Cornwall.

MEN-AN-TOL
Morvah

On the high moors two miles east of Morvah is a round holed stone, four feet in diameter, flanked by two upright stones, each about four-and-a-half feet high. A fourth fallen stone lies nearby. The stones are thought to date from the Bronze Age but their purpose is unknown. To confuse matters, one, at least, has been moved in recent times. The Men-an-Tol, meaning 'stone of the hole', is a circular granite slab pierced by a hole about twenty inches in diameter. It is also known as the 'Crick Stone' and was believed to possess magical and curative powers. In a field, 300 yards north-west, is an inscribed standing stone known as Men Scryfa or 'Stone with Writing'. It is about six feet tall, with an inscription reading RIALOBRAN CUNOVAL FIL, meaning 'Rialobran, son of Cunoval', and dates from the fifth or sixth century AD. On the hill to the east is an ancient stone circle known as the Nine Maidens. All the stones are reached by a signposted track running north-east from Bosullow Common on the Trevowhan (near Morvah) to Madron road. On the hilltop to the south-west are the remains of Chun Castle, an Iron Age hillfort constructed of stone.

ENGINE HOUSES
Bottalack

Perched on the rugged cliffs at the Crowns, some thirty feet above the Atlantic, are the remains of the engine houses of the famous Bottalack mine, near St Just. One of the oldest tin mines in Cornwall, it was described in *Murray's Handbook* of 1859: 'The Crown Engine, well known for the wild exposure of its position, was lowered down a cliff of 200 ft. to the ledge it now occupies, for the purpose of enabling the miner to penetrate beneath the bed of the Atlantic.' A sloping shaft was driven out a third of a mile under the sea and, while working, a miner could hear 'the booming of the waves and the grating of stones as they are rolled to and fro over his head'. Young Prince Arthur visited the mine in 1862. Until it closed in 1914, Bottalack was worked for copper, tin and arsenic. The building above the pumping engine house held a whim engine for winding ore to the surface. They were restored in 1984–5. The nearby Levant Mine, closed in 1930, extended for more than a mile out to sea and reached a record depth of 2100 feet below the sea bed. The beam whim or winding engine, built in 1840 and now restored, is the only one working under steam in Cornwall. It is owned by the National Trust.

CAPE CORNWALL
St Just

Long thought to be the most
westerly point in England, Cape
Cornwall lies on the Atlantic coast
about a mile west of the old mining
town of St Just. Formerly owned
by Francis Oats – who died in
1918 and built Porthledden House
nearby – the Cape was purchased
for the nation by H. J. Heinz Co.
Ltd and was presented to the
National Trust in 1987. The area
was mined extensively for tin and
copper from about 1600. The
chimney stack crowning the
promontory belonged to the Cape
Cornwall Mine, opened in 1836,
and was renovated in 1986. It was
erected to improve the draught to
the boiler house, now converted
into a private house. The mine
manager or 'captain' lived in the
square-built house close by. In the
privately owned field below the
Cape are the remains of a small
medieval chapel, known as St
Helen's or St Catherine's oratory,
possibly standing on an earlier
Celtic site. Due south of the Cape
is Priest's Cove where, for
centuries, local fishermen have
launched their small boats. About
a mile south-west of the Cape are
two jagged slate rocks known as
The Brisons, said to resemble
General De Gaulle lying in his
bath. They have claimed many
ships over the years.

ARMED KNIGHT
Land's End

The westernmost point in
mainland England and Wales,
Land's End is a magnet for
tourists. The vertical grey granite
cliffs, on average about 100 feet
high, stand against the full erosive
force of the Atlantic. Classical
writers called the Land's End
peninsula 'Belerion' or 'the seat of
storms'. The seas around the
jagged coastline are notoriously
dangerous for shipping, among the
wrecks they have claimed being the
Torrey Canyon supertanker which
ran aground on the Seven Stones
reef in 1967. The Longships
Lighthouse in the photograph is
about a mile and a half offshore.
On the seaward side the light is
white while on the landward side it
is ruby red. The first lighthouse
was built in 1795 and replaced in
1873. J. M. W. Turner painted a
picture of the lighthouse in 1834,
which John Ruskin greatly
admired. The lost land of Lyonesse
(thought to be identical with
Liones, the home of Tristan) is
said to lie beneath the sea between
the Isles of Scilly and the
mainland. Among the attractions
and exhibits at Land's End is the
Last Labyrinth, 'a multi-sensory
experience'. There is also a hotel
and the First and Last House.

MINACK THEATRE
Porthcurno

Perched on a grassy gully between rugged granite cliffs east of Porthcurno Bay, the Minack open-air theatre was created almost single-handedly by the landowner Rowena Cade. The first performance staged in the Greek-style amphitheatre was Shakespeare's *The Tempest* in 1932. Today the 750-seat, fully equipped theatre (with an Exhibition Centre telling the story of its founder) is administered by a Trust. Against a memorable backdrop of sea and sky, performances of a wide range of plays are staged throughout the summer. Recorded on the back of many of the terraced concrete seats are the names and dates of past productions. On the opposite side of the bay, on the distant headland, are the earthwork remains of an Iron Age cliff castle dating from 500 BC. Also on the headland is the famous Logan Rock, a large rounded boulder which was once so precisely balanced that it would rock at the slightest push. Weighing over sixty tons, it was deliberately dislodged in 1824 by Lieutenant Hugh Colvill Goldsmith and some of the crew of *HMS Nimble*. Although the Admiralty made Goldsmith replace it, the balance has never been the same.

MOUSEHOLE

On Sunday 23 July 1595 four Spanish galleys, which had sailed from their base in Brittany, landed 400 men at the tiny fishing village of Mousehole (pronounced Mouzel). It is said that Jenkin Keigwin, the village squire, made a heroic stand against the invaders, but was killed by a cannonball. The Spanish burnt Mousehole and the church at nearby Paul, before moving on to attack Newlyn and Penzance. The only house to survive in Mousehole was the manor house, later to become the Keigwin Arms and now a private house. It has a porch with a room above supported on granite columns. Mousehole, three miles south of Penzance, has one of Cornwall's oldest harbours, with a pier first built *c.* 1393. A new pier was constructed in 1861. Just outside the harbour entrance is St Clement's Isle, referred to in the village's former name of Porth Enys or 'Island Port'. Dolly Pentreath, reputedly the last person to speak the Cornish language, came from the village. She died in 1777 and her memorial can be seen in the outer wall of Paul churchyard. On 19 December 1981 the Penlee lifeboat, the *Solomon Browne*, was involved in a tragic incident in which its eight-man crew – all men from Mousehole – were drowned.

PENZANCE
from Newlyn Harbour

Penzance was granted its first market charter in 1514. In July 1595, together with Mousehole and Newlyn, it was burned to the ground by Spanish raiders. The town had been rebuilt by 1614 but was sacked by the Parliamentarians in 1646. Charles II confirmed its charter in 1663. In the same year it became the chief coinage town (see page 33), retaining this position until 1838, for tin produced west of Cambourne, and thus flourished on the Penwith tin-mining industry. The arrival of the railway from London in 1859 led to its development as a holiday resort. Humphrey Davy, inventor of the miner's safety lamp, was born in the town in 1778. St Mary's church, rising above the harbour, dates from 1832–5. Penzance maintains regular boat and helicopter services to the Isles of Scilly. Newlyn is Cornwall's largest fishing port. Its harbour was built at the end of the nineteenth century and encloses a fifteenth-century pier. Further expansion of fishing facilities, including a new pier, took place in the 1980s. The Irish painter Stanhope Forbes (1857–1947) first visited Newlyn in 1884, founding the Newlyn School of painting in 1899.

ST MICHAEL'S MOUNT
Marazion

St Michael's Mount is thought to be the ancient island of 'Ictis' mentioned by the Greek historian Diodorus in 70 BC, which exported tin to France. After St Michael's appearance to two fishermen in AD 495, the Mount became an important religious site for pilgrims. Edward the Confessor founded a Benedictine monastery on the granite rock. After the Norman Conquest it became a possession of Mont St Michel in Normandy and in 1135 was elevated to a priory. In 1424 Henry VI confirmed the grant of the priory to Syon Abbey, Twickenham. The first 'Arch-Priest', William Morton, built the harbour and 500-foot-long stone causeway linking the island to the mainland at low tide. The priory was dissolved *c.*1535 and the Mount became a fortress (the castle dates from the fourteenth century). A Royalist stronghold during the Civil War, it was captured by the Parliamentarians in 1646. In 1659 the Mount was bought by Colonel John St Aubyn, and the St Aubyn family have lived in the castle ever since. The third Lord St Levan granted the island to the National Trust in 1954. Traces of a submerged forest, dating from *c.*1700 BC, have been revealed at very low tides.

LOE BAR
Porthleven

Loe Pool, the largest natural freshwater lake in Cornwall, is separated from the sea by the shingle bank of Loe Bar (midway between Porthleven and Gunwalloe). The Pool was originally the estuary of the River Cober which flows through the former port of Helston, two miles inland. By the thirteenth century the Bar was fully formed and access to the sea was cut off. The shingle is mainly composed of flint. As there are no land deposits of this stone along the southern Cornish coast, it is thought that it originates from somewhere offshore. Over the centuries, to prevent parts of Helston flooding, the Bar has occasionally been breached. However, it seals itself again quite quickly. Loe Pool is reputed to be the lake in which Sir Bedivere cast King Arthur's sword, Excalibur (Dozmary Pool on Bodmin Moor is an alternative site). Local superstition warns that the Pool claims a victim every seven years. Many ships have been wrecked on the Bar, including *HMS Anson* on 29 December 1807. As a result of the lives lost, Henry Trengrouse of Helston, who watched the tragedy helplessly from the shore, invented the rocket life-saving apparatus.

CADGWITH COVE
The Lizard

The fishing village of Cadgwith, on the east coast of the Lizard peninsula, lies in a small sheltered cove consisting of two tiny beaches divided by the Todden promontory. The boats, winched up onto the shingle beach above the high tide mark, are used mainly for lobster and crab fishing. Before the pilchard shoals ceased to come inshore in about 1900, the villagers depended on the fish (and smuggling) for their livelihood. The old pilchard cellars have now been converted into holiday accommodation. Some of the stone cottages are thatched, their eaves chained down to prevent the roofs blowing away in severe gales. High on the cliffs to the north is a small hut with a chimney, built in the nineteenth century as a coastguard's watch house. It is sometimes referred to as a 'huer's hut' because from there a huer, or lookout, kept watch for shoals of pilchards. There was a lifeboat station at Cadgwith from 1867 to 1963. Just south of the cove is the Devil's Frying Pan, a large hole in the cliff, thought to have been formed by the collapse of a sea cave. A mile up the coast, at Poltesco, are the remains of an old serpentine stone works.

MULLION COVE
The Lizard

The tiny harbour at Mullion Cove (anciently called Porth Mellin) was built between 1893 and 1895. After the decline in the pilchard shoals at the end of the nineteenth century, the fishermen built up a successful crab and lobster business. Mullion had a lifeboat station from 1867 to 1909. The cove, harbour and Mullion Island belong to the National Trust. The village of Mullion is about a mile inland. The church is noted for its early sixteenth-century carved bench ends. In *Mullyon*, published in 1875, the Revd E. G. Harvey, vicar of Mullion, relates many stories of smuggling in the area. It was a 'fair trade' that benefited the whole community. Apparently it was rare for those who were caught to be punished, except with the confiscation of the stolen goods. To the north, at Angrouse Cliffs, Poldhu, is a granite monument to Guglielmo Marconi, who transmitted the first wireless signal across the Atlantic from there on 12 December 1901. The first Satellite Earth Station was established in 1962, just over two miles away at Goonhilly.

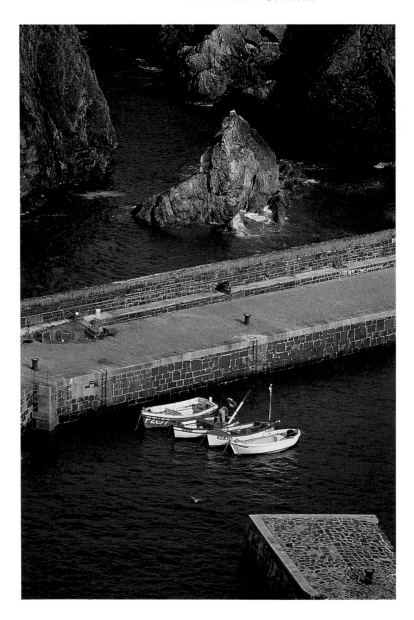

LIZARD POINT

'The neighbourhood is sadly infested with wreckers. When the news of a wreck flies round the coast, thousands of people are instantly collected near the fatal spot . . . The moment the vessel touches the shore she is considered fair plunder.' So wrote Revd G. C. Smith in *The Wreckers; or a Tour of Benevolence from St Michael's Mount to Lizard Point* (1817). More ships have been wrecked on the jagged rocks and reefs off Lizard Point than anywhere else on the south coast of England. Sir John Killigrew, whose family was notorious for piracy and smuggling, erected the first light here in 1619. Perhaps, by preventing ships from going down at the Lizard, he hoped they would founder nearer his home at Falmouth, where he owned the wrecking rights. Whatever his motives, Killigrew's light met with fierce opposition from two sources: Trinity House and the local inhabitants, who feared that it would put an end to their source of 'fair plunder'. The light was abandoned in 1623. The present twin-towered lighthouse was erected in 1752. A single flashing light was installed in the eastern tower in 1903 and the western one discontinued. It now controls and monitors all the unmanned lighthouses in the area.

Truro and Central Cornwall

TOWANROATH ENGINE HOUSE
St Agnes

On the hills and cliffs to the west of St Agnes are many impressive remains of past mining activity. The village was the centre of a mining community from the sixteenth century until the 1920s. During its heyday there were over 100 tin and copper mines in the area, employing over 1000 miners. Although none of the mines are working today, among the most noted were Wheal Kitty, Wheal Friendly, Blue Hills and Wheal Coates. The Towanroath engine house, standing on the cliffs below the ruins of the Wheal Coates winding and stamps engine houses, is about a mile south of St Agnes Head, near the Chapel Porth cliffs. Although earliest records state that the Wheal Coates mine was working in 1692, copper and tin ore were dug from the cliff face much earlier. Despite evidence to the contrary, tradition says that the Phoenicians traded for tin from St Agnes over 2300 years ago. Wheal Coates closed *c.* 1889, but attempts were made to rework the mine in 1910–14. The Towanroath engine house was restored by the National Trust in 1973. At low tide it is possible to view the workings of the Towanroath Shaft from a sea cave.

In 1602 Truro was one of four 'coinage' towns in Cornwall, the others being Lostwithiel, Liskeard and Helston. It was at these official stannary centres, originally twice a year, that the miners had to bring their tin to be weighed, or 'coigned', when a corner was cut from each ingot to test it for purity; they were then stamped and valued, following which the coinage dues were paid. As a port, Truro became an important centre for commerce and industry, flourishing particularly on the export of tin.

The production of tin in Devon and Cornwall dates back to prehistoric times. The early tinners laboured not underground in mines but on the surface, uncovering the alluvial ore by streaming, a method of extracting the heavy pebbles of cassiterite (found in the beds of rivers) by washing the lighter waste material away. In places where substantial deposits of tin had accumulated it would be dug out. As the ore is usually associated with granites, most of the tin workings were concentrated around the granite outcrops of Dartmoor, Bodmin Moor, Carnmenellis (south of Redruth), Hensbarrow Downs (St Austell) and the Land's End peninsula. When the alluvial deposits were exhausted, the tin-streamers turned their attention away from the valley bottoms to the upland veins or lodes from which the ore originated.

The tin-mining districts of the West Country were known as stannaries, but the exact origins of the system are uncertain. Some form of stannary organization was in existence during Anglo-Saxon times, with records of stannary courts being held in the tenth century, when dues on all tin mined had to be paid to the Crown. There is no mention of tin production in the *Domesday Book* of 1086, possibly because it was considered to be royal property. The Pipe Rolls of 1155–6, however, clearly show that the tin industry was not only flourishing but also expanding. Most of the tin at this time was produced in Dartmoor, despite the fact that it was more abundant in Cornwall.

By 1201, when King John granted a charter confirming the rights and privileges of the tinners, the industry had become so important that the stannaries were virtually self-governing states. As such, the tinners were exempt from common law and ordinary taxes, having their own stannary laws, customs, courts and gaol. John's charter – together with the 1305 charter of Edward I, which replaced the previous system of taxation with coinage dues – formed the basic structure of the stannaries until they were abolished in the

WALSINGHAM PLACE AND THE CATHEDRAL
Truro

The cathedral city and administrative capital of Cornwall, Truro lies at the confluence of the rivers Allen and Kenwyn at the head of the Truro River (merging with other rivers, including the Fal, it eventually flows into the English Channel at Falmouth). The Normans built a castle at Truro on Castle Hill of which nothing now remains. During the Middle Ages the city was a stannary town and flourishing port with jurisdiction over the whole estuary. Falmouth disputed the ancient right in 1709 and won. Thereafter, together with the silting up of the estuary, Truro declined as a port. It became a fashionable centre during Georgian times and was granted city status in 1877 by Queen Victoria. The cathedral, begun in 1880, was designed by John Loughborough Pearson in the Early English Gothic style and completed in 1910, after his death. The south aisle of the old sixteenth-century parish church of St Mary was incorporated into the structure, and a chapter house was added in 1967. High Cross, to the west of the cathedral, was formerly the site of the cattle market. The terraced houses in Walsingham Place are Georgian.

nineteenth century. There were four stannaries in Cornwall, Blackmore (Hensbarrow Downs and St Austell), Foweymore (Bodmin Moor), Tywarnhaile (St Agnes, Redruth and Truro area) and Penwith and Kerrier (Land's End and Helston area), and four in Devon, Chagford, Tavistock, Ashburton and Plympton. Towns in each of the districts were officially appointed as coinage centres.

It is thought that the first attempts at mining an actual lode or vein were made in the coastal districts of Cornwall, where the ore was exposed in the cliffs and could be exploited by driving in levels or galleries. Similar methods would also have been used wherever a lode outcropped on a hillside or in a valley. Most tin and copper lodes, rather than running horizontally, slope upwards or downwards. If a shaft was to be driven below the natural water level, some form of artificial drainage was essential to prevent flooding. According to Richard Carew's *Survey of Cornwall*, published in 1602, some of the mines had reached a depth of 'forty or fifty fathom' (300 feet).

The discovery of rich veins of copper in the early eighteenth century led to a boom in the West Country mining industry which lasted until the 1860s, when the mines were forced to close because of severe foreign competition. As a direct result of the collapse of the great copper mines, many Cornish miners emigrated, particularly to the Americas, Australia and South Africa, where their skills were in demand. The Industrial Revolution brought dramatic changes to the mining industry. As the mines grew deeper, it became increasingly difficult to keep them free of water. The invention of the Newcomen engine (first erected in Staffordshire in 1712 and replaced by James Watt's steam pumping engine some sixty-five years later) brought significant improvements in mining efficiency and profitability. The development of the famous Cornish pumping engine, which dominated the industry from the 1820s, was due to the efforts of Richard Trevithick and other local engineers. In the middle of the nineteenth century the mines of Cornwall accounted for three quarters of the world's copper and almost half of its tin. Although tin continued to be mined after the copper boom had finished, it too suffered a decline, albeit gradual, and by the 1920s most of the mines had been abandoned. Today, the principal industry in Cornwall is the production of china clay, mainly centred around Hensbarrow Downs and St Austell.

BEDRUTHAN STEPS
Bedruthan

The railway line to Newquay was opened to passengers in 1876 and the town quickly became a popular holiday resort. One of the attractions for the Victorian tourist was a five-mile carriage trip north to Bedruthan to view the wave- and weather-worn stacks, most of which have names. Samaritan Island, is named after the Liverpool brig *Samaritan* which was driven against the rock in a storm and wrecked in 1846. At the time local people are reputed to have said: 'The Good Samaritan came ashore, to feed the rich and clothe the poor.' Queen Bess Rock, which bore a resemblance to Elizabeth I wearing her crown, ruff and farthingale, lost its top in the early 1980s. The sandy beach is dangerous for bathing. The 'Steps' have been variously thought to refer to the whole beach, the stacks, the ladders used to reach the mine workings or the steep cliff staircase down to the beach. The National Trust shop at the top of the crumbling slate cliffs was originally the count house (or offices) for the Carnewas Mine. The earthwork castles of Redcliff and Park Head date from the Iron Age.

CRANTOCK BEACH
near Newquay

Crantock Beach, backed by sand dunes rising to the grassy plateau of Rushy Green, lies between the rocky headlands of Pentire Point West and Pentire Point East. The ancient city of Langarrow (or Languna), with its seven churches, is reputed to be buried beneath the sand. At the entrance to a cave on the west side of the beach – accessible at low tide – a flat rock has been carved with the outline of a woman and the words, now almost illegible: 'Mar not my face but let me be / Secure in this lone cavern by the sea / Let the wild waves around me roar / Kissing my lips for evermore.' Running along the east side of the beach is the Gannel, the tidal outlet of the River Gannel which rises on Newlyn Downs, south of St Newlyn East. The estuary was used by shipping until the end of the nineteenth century, when the narrow channel began to silt up with sand. Newquay nearby, with its sandy beaches, rocky headlands and sheltered harbour, is one of the most popular resorts in Cornwall. Known as 'Kaye' in 1439 and 'New Kaye' by 1602, the town was a market and lead-mining centre, seafaring port, fishing community and smugglers' haunt.

CHAPEL ROCK AND DROSKYN POINT
Perranporth

The holiday resort of Perranporth lies on the north Cornwall coast some six miles south-west of Newquay. Chapel Rock, once known as Chapel Angarder, was the site of a Christian chapel belonging to the ancient manor of Reen. The cliffs around Droskyn Point bear evidence of mine workings dating from the eighteenth century, when tin, copper and other ores were extracted. The archway in the photograph is a natural formation. North of Perranporth the cliffs gave way to a three-mile stretch of firm sand, behind which are extensive dunes. Buried amongst the dunes (or towans) is the lost church of St Piran, dating from the fifth or sixth century, which was excavated in 1835. A sign nearby claims that it is 'the earliest Christian building in England'. The church has now been reburied, preserved within a concrete shell, and the site is marked by a small stone. St Piran (or Perran), who is said to have lived to the age of 206, is reputed to have sailed from Ireland to Cornwall on a millstone in the fifth century. Two crosses can also be found nearby, one of which dates from *c.* 800. Also in the vicinity are the foundations of a pre-Norman church of *c.* 1000.

STIPPY STAPPY
St Agnes

The village of St Agnes, which lies at the top of a wooded valley in the shadow of the 629-foot hill of St Agnes Beacon, was once the centre of a thriving mining industry, noted for its high-quality tin. Ore was shipped from the quay at Trevaunance Porth, less than a mile to the north, and commodities such as coal and timber were brought in. The row of stepped terraced cottages below the spired church, which stands on a steep footpath called 'Stippy Stappy', was originally owned by the shipping companies whose vessels traded in the harbour. To accommodate the congregation, greatly enlarged by the mining population, the church of St Agnes was entirely rebuilt in 1848. The miners were paid in the counting house, a large room in the St Agnes Hotel, originally called 'The Commercial'. John Opie (1761–1807), a self-taught artist known as the 'Cornish Wonder', was born in Harmony Cottage, between Mithian and Trevellas, just to the east of St Agnes. Some of his paintings are in the Royal Cornwall Museum, Truro, and the National Portrait Gallery, London. On the summit of St Agnes Beacon are the remains of several Bronze Age barrows. Legend says that the hill was the home of the giant known as Bolster, who was killed by St Agnes.

CARN BREA CASTLE
Redruth

Carn Brea Castle stands on the top of a 738-foot-high granite outcrop overlooking the mining towns of Redruth and Cambourne. Thought to have been an Elizabethan hunting lodge, the sham fortress is now a restaurant. Further along the ridge is a monument, erected in 1836, dedicated to Francis, Lord de Dunstanville (1757–1835), one of the wealthy mine-owning Bassets of Tehidy. The site was a Neolithic hilltop settlement and later an Iron Age fortress. Excavations have yielded Stone Age arrowheads, Bronze Age axe heads and Celtic and Roman coins. The surrounding landscape, once described as Cornwall's 'Black Country', is cluttered with the remains of numerous abandoned copper and tin mines, known locally as 'knackt bals'. The famous Dolcoath Mine was not only the county's premier tin mine, it was also the deepest at 3300 feet. It closed in 1920. Richard Trevithick, noted for developing the high-pressure non-condensing steam pumping engine and the world's first steam railway locomotive, was born at Illogan near Redruth in 1771. The Redruth home of the Scottish inventor William Murdoch was the first house in Britain to be lit by coal gas (1792).

GWENNAP PIT
Busveal

In 1738 John Wesley, founder of the Methodist movement, set out to travel the length and breadth of Britain proclaiming the good news of salvation by faith. He arrived in Cornwall in 1743 and soon found himself preaching in the heavily populated tin- and copper-mining area around Redruth. He first preached in Gwennap Pit in 1762. In his *Journal* he wrote: 'the wind was so high at five that I could not stand in the usual place at Gwennap. But at a small distance was a hollow capable of containing many thousand people. I stood on one side of this amphitheatre toward the top, with people beneath and on all sides.' He came here eighteen times between 1762 and 1789, claiming to preach to congregations of twenty to thirty thousand. The pit (probably created by mining subsidence) continued to be used by Methodist preachers after Wesley's death in 1791. It was remodelled as a formal stepped amphitheatre in 1806 and is still used for occasional services. Adjoining the pit is the Busveal Chapel and Visitor Centre.

FALMOUTH

Originally a cluster of fishermen's cottages called Pennycomequick and Smithick, Falmouth became a flourishing port and mail packet station at the end of the seventeenth century. This was due to the Killigrew family, who had originally made their wealth from smuggling, privateering and piracy. In a report dated *c.* 1600 Sir Walter Raleigh brought attention to the strategic importance and commercial potential of the area. By then the mouth of the Fal was protected by Henry VIII's castles of St Mawes and Pendennis. Sir John Killigrew saw the possibilities of developing the site into a prosperous town. It grew quickly, and during the Civil War became a Royalist stronghold. A market was established in 1652 and, at about the same time, Sir Peter Killigrew engineered the removal of the Custom House from Penryn. His support for the Royalist cause was acknowledged by Charles II in 1661 when the place was incorporated as a town and named Falmouth. It was the second busiest port in Britain until sail gave way to steam at the end of the nineteenth century. The parish church, built in 1662, is dedicated to King Charles the Martyr.

PENDENNIS CASTLE
Falmouth

Fearing a French invasion of England in 1539, Henry VIII started to build or strengthen a chain of fortresses and blockhouses around the coast facing Europe. Work began on the castles of St Mawes and Pendennis in 1540 and was completed in 1545. Strategically sited on either side of the entrance to the Carrick Roads, they were erected not for the protection of Falmouth (which did not exist) but for the defence and protection of Penryn. Pendennis, derived from Pen Dinas meaning 'the headland with a fort', was erected on land leased from the local landowner, John Killigrew, who became the first governor. (The Little Dennis Fort, on the shoreline at the very end of the headland, was built at the same time.) The original fortress was completely enclosed by a new one, built in 1598–9. It was a Royalist stronghold during the Civil War, and its 900-strong garrison under Colonel John Arundell surrendered to the Parliamentarians in 1646 after a five-month siege. They were granted full honours of war and allowed to march from the castle 'drums beating, colours flying, trumpets sounding'. Pendennis is now in the care of English Heritage.

THE MEETING HOUSE
Come-to-Good

The hamlet of Come-to-Good, some three miles south of Truro, is thought to derive its name from 'Cwm-ty-coit' meaning 'the dwelling in the wooded coombe'. It is noted for its thatched and whitewashed Quaker Meeting House, built with cob walls in 1710. Originally rectangular in design, the building was later extended at both ends, the east end providing stabling for the worshippers' horses. The 'loft', supported by two wooden posts, was added in 1717, dividing the inside of the building almost in half. Although the house is now secluded, an old route from Truro to Falmouth once passed its door, leading to the ferry crossing of Restronguet Creek at Penpol. It is thought that the early Quaker travelling preachers George Bewley and James Miers may have used the route in 1656. The following year there was a large Quaker meeting 'near Penryn'. The Quakers or 'Society of Friends' were persecuted during the latter part of the Commonwealth and also after the Restoration of Charles II in 1660. The persecution of Quakers, and Puritans in general, gradually disappeared after the Toleration Act of 1689.

PARISH CHURCH
St Just in Roseland

Overlooking Carrick Roads, on the Roseland Peninsula, is the tiny hamlet of St Just in Roseland. The church, set beside a small creek, stands on the site of a sixth-century Celtic foundation. The present church, dedicated to St Just, dates from the mid-thirteenth century. The slate tower was erected in the early fifteenth century, together with much of the south side of the building. Bad restoration in the nineteenth century stripped the interior of most of its ancient furnishings, including the old pews. The churchyard, rising steeply behind the church, is full of exotic sub-tropical trees and plants, and is considered to be one of the most beautiful in the country. Both lych gates date from 1632. The fifty-five granite stones that line the main path down to the church were placed by the Revd Humfrey Davis, who was rector from 1901 to 1930. The large flat tombstone of Mathilda Jenking (1698–1750) tells the story of one of her fourteen children who was drowned at sea. St Just's is also the parish church for St Mawes.

VICTORY STEPS
St Mawes

The former port and fishing village of St Mawes lies on the Roseland Peninsula at the western side of the Fal estuary, opposite Falmouth. The harbour, now a popular yachting haven, lies in the shelter of the mouth of the Percuil River. Nevertheless, the quay, first built of stone in 1536, has suffered from storm damage over the centuries. The entrance to the Victory Inn, dated 1792, is on Victory Steps. Some twenty yards higher up the street, next to Rockwell Cottage, is a holy well dating from the sixth century. Its stone arch, erected in the fifteenth century and rebuilt in 1939, is dedicated to the Welshman St Mawes, who lived here in the sixth century. At the south-western end of the town is St Mawes Castle, built by Henry VIII in 1540–45. Its purpose, with Pendennis Castle, was to protect the mouth of the Fal (or Carrick Roads) against invasion. It is designed on a clover-leaf plan with three lower bastions enclosing a round central tower or keep. The castle was augmented by a smaller fort on the shoreline to the south-west. St Mawes, with nineteen guns, was intended to be an artillery fort rather than a castle.

ROUND HOUSE AND OLD THATCH COTTAGE
Veryan

There are five, whitewashed round houses in Veryan, two at each end of the village and one behind the school. The latter has a tiled roof while the others are thatched. All are surmounted by crosses, and tradition says that the houses had no north opening by which the Devil could enter and no corners for him to hide in. They were built in the early nineteenth century by the Revd Jeremiah Trist, who got the idea from a friend, Charles Penrose of Ethy in St Winnow. A ground plan of the houses, published in 1811, depicts a single-storey building with two bedrooms, a kitchen, pantry and wood store. The houses are built of cob (a mixture of clay, earth and straw) on stone foundations. Provided that it has 'a good hat and shoes', a cob house is remarkably weatherproof. Today, they are privately owned and have had a second storey and extensions added. At the rear of the Old Thatch Cottage (once the White Hart inn and a saddlery) are the Veryan Galleries. The village has two holy wells. The church of St Symphorian is unusual in that the slate tower was built on the south side. Veryan is some six miles south-east of Truro.

PARISH CHURCH
Probus

The church at Probus is built of Cornish granite from St Stephen-in-Brannel and stands on a fifth-century Celtic Christian site. A Saxon church, founded *c.* 930 by Athelstan, King of Wessex, was recorded at Probus in the *Domesday Book*. The present church dates from *c.* 1450. The richly ornamented tower, the tallest in Cornwall at 125 feet 10 inches, was erected in about 1523. Inside the church is a memorial to Thomas Hawkins, who died in 1766. The Hawkins family lived at Trewithen, about a mile to the east of the village. Trewithen House, surrounded by parkland, was built for them in 1715–40 by Thomas Edwards of Greenwich, with later additions by Sir Robert Taylor. The gardens, created by George Johnstone, are planted with a splendid collection of magnolias, camellias and rhododendrons. The house and gardens are open to the public. Sir Christopher Hawkins of Trewithen, together with the mayor of Grampound and others, was accused and acquitted of corrupt practices in 1808. He was said to have been so mean that he had 'a large park without deer, a large cellar without beer and a large house without cheer'.

ST MICHAEL'S CHAPEL
Roche Rock

In the midst of Roche rocks – a sixty-foot-high mass of granite, rich in crystals of white quartz and black tourmaline – are the roofless remains of St Michael's chapel, built as a hermitage (with a chapel above) in 1409. The physical effort involved in raising the huge granite blocks which make up the building remains, as Pevsner said, 'a feat to be wondered at'. Some 680 feet above sea level, the chapel stands on the northern edge of Hensbarrow Downs overlooking the white pyramids and spoil heaps of china clay country. Tradition says that the rock was once the home of St Gonand, to whom the restored church in Roche village, nearby, is dedicated. One of the holy men who occupied the cell, according to legend, was tormented by the troubled spirit of John Tregeagle, a lawyer who had sold his soul to the Devil and was condemned to haunt the wild moors and coastlands, forever plagued by demons. Fleeing from Dozmary Pool during a ferocious storm, he was chased by the demons to Roche Rock, where he attempted to seek sanctuary by thrusting his head through the chapel window. Only by the use of magic spells could his terrible screams be silenced.

MEVAGISSEY

The old fishing port of Mevagissey on the south coast, five miles south of St Austell, was once famous for its pilchards and was known as 'Fishy Gissy'. During the eighteenth and nineteenth centuries pilchards, cured in salt, were exported to Italy and the West Indies. They were also supplied in large quantities to the Royal Navy, who called them 'Mevagissey Ducks', and their oil was used for lamps. The prosperity of the port was supplemented by smuggling. The narrow streets of colour-washed houses and cottages climb up the steep hillsides above the harbour, which has an inner and outer quay. A monkey, washed ashore from a wrecked French ship during the Napoleonic wars, was reputedly hanged by the locals who feared that it was a spy. The church of St Peter, in what was originally the separate settlement of Lamorrick or Lavorrick, is mainly fifteenth-century. Having become ruinous, the upper part of the medieval tower was demolished in the seventeenth century but was rebuilt in 1887. Inside the church, the memorials to Otwell Hill (d. 1617) and Lewis Dart (d. 1632) are of particular interest. Mevagissey is named after St Meva (possibly Mewan) and St Issey.

FOWEY ESTUARY
from Bodinnick

St Catherine's Castle (on the right in the photograph) was one of a chain of castles built on the orders of Henry VIII to protect the south coast from French invasion. It stands on the western entrance to Fowey harbour and is now in the care of English Heritage. On the opposite headland are the remains of a blockhouse built after the French invaded Fowey in 1457. The River Fowey rises on Bodmin Moor and flows through Lostwithiel to enter the sea beyond the historic town of Fowey. Tin ore was shipped from there to France until the trade was halted in the fourteenth century because of the Hundred Years' War. Today china clay is exported by ships (some over 10,000 tons) to all parts of the world from the docks north of Fowey. During the fifteenth century the town was a centre for piracy. Fowey was the 'Troy Town' of Sir Arthur Quiller-Couch's novel *The Astonishing History of Troy Town* (1888) and the 'little grey sea town' in Kenneth Grahame's *The Wind in the Willows* (1908). A mile or so north-west of Fowey is the Tristan Stone (formerly called the Longstone). The sixth-century inscribed stone, now set in a modern plinth, was originally sited two miles further north, near Castle Dore.

BAPTISTRY
Menacuddle

Cornwall is the 'Land of Saints'. It is said that there are more saints in the county than there are in heaven. Countless parishes, churches, towns, villages and holy wells have been dedicated to the Christian missionaries who came to this south-western peninsula from Wales, Ireland and Brittany, chiefly during the fifth and sixth centuries. St Mewan, accompanied by his disciple St Austell, journeyed from Wales to Brittany by way of Cornwall in the sixth century. The two adjoining parishes of St Mewan and St Austell are named after them. St Austell is reputed to have used the holy well at Menacuddle (meaning 'rock well') for his baptisms and ministrations. Menacuddle lies by a small stream and waterfall less than a mile north of the old market town of St Austell, on the road to Trethowel. The small granite baptistry which now stands on the site dates from the fifteenth century.

RESTORMEL CASTLE
Lostwithiel

Restormel Castle stands on a commanding hilltop site, overlooking the River Fowey, about a mile north of the medieval town of Lostwithiel. First built *c.* 1100 by Baldwin Fitz Turstin, with a circular shell keep dating from *c.* 1200, it is the best preserved Norman motte and bailey castle in Cornwall. In 1270 it became the property of Richard, Earl of Cornwall, and passed to his son Edmund two years later. Further rebuilding took place within the 125-foot-diameter keep during Edmund's ownership. Since 1299, when Edmund died, the castle has belonged to the Duchy of Cornwall. It was visited by Edward the Black Prince in 1354 and 1365. By the middle of the sixteenth century the castle, which stood in a deer park, had been abandoned. Leland noted *c.* 1540: 'There is a castle on a hill in this park where sometimes the Earls of Cornwall lay. The base court is sore defaced. The fair large dungeon yet standeth.' The keep was occupied by the Parliamentary army of Lord Essex during the Civil War but was captured by Sir Richard Grenville in 1644. It is now in the care of English Heritage.

Tintagel and North-Eastern Cornwall

HARBOUR MOUTH
Boscastle

In the days of sail, entering and leaving the narrow tortuous inlet at Boscastle was a difficult and dangerous manoeuvre. As a commercial port Boscastle reached its peak during the nineteenth century, importing coal and limestone from South Wales and wine, timber and corn from Bristol. Exports included Delabole slate, china clay and locally mined manganese ore. In about 1540 Leland noted that the town was 'very filthy' and 'ill-kept' with 'a poor havenet of no certain safeguard'. The ruinous inner quay was rebuilt by Sir Richard Grenville in 1587 while the outer breakwater, erected *c.* 1820, was destroyed by a mine in 1941 and rebuilt in 1962. Beneath Penally Point is a natural blowhole known as the Devil's Bellows, which when wind and tide are right blows a horizontal waterspout partway across the harbour mouth (this generally occurs about an hour either side of low tide). On the summit of the 317-foot-high promontory of Willapark, the site of an Iron Age cliff fort, is a whitewashed tower once used as a coastguard's lookout. Inland, on Forrabury Common, are the 'stitches', a Celtic strip cultivation system.

Legend says that King Arthur was conceived at Tintagel Castle towards the end of the fifth century AD, though historians and archaeologists maintain that the clifftop ruins were not built until the twelfth century. Recent excavations at the site have, however, uncovered the foundations of about fifty small buildings of a much earlier date: was this an ancient monastic settlement, or the fortress of a Celtic chieftain? Whatever the findings may be, the general consensus is that Tintagel was a site of special significance in Britain. It has been established that during the sixth century the great natural citadel was a place inhabited by kings, that it dealt in long-distance trade, particularly with the eastern Mediterranean, that it was connected with Christianity, and that the cemetery of Tintagel church was an important burial site. Although many of these elements are echoed in the Arthurian story, there is no hard evidence to link the site with Arthur. The 'Once and Future King' seems forever shrouded in mystery.

Arthur is one of the most enduring and enigmatic figures in British myth and legend. Today historians generally accept that the numerous and often fabulous stories about Arthur are based on a real person, a great Celtic hero and military leader who existed in the late fifth and early sixth centuries. After his death Arthur became a symbol of hope against oppression, especially in predominantly Celtic regions like Wales, southern Scotland, Cornwall and Brittany. He lived during a particularly turbulent and bloody period in British history – shortly after the Roman legions had been withdrawn, and during the struggle for domination between the Celts or Britons and the invading Anglo-Saxons, Picts and Scots.

Stories of Arthur's exploits were essentially passed on by word of mouth. In the process, however, they were expanded and elaborated, drawing in elements of folklore, myth and legend. The earliest written reference to Arthur's name occurs in a ninth-century manuscript, *Historia Brittonum*, compiled by Nennius, a Welsh cleric from Bangor. It says that Arthur was victorious in twelve battles, culminating in the battle of Badon. The later *Annales Cambriae* (Annals of Wales) mentions the battle of Badon again and adds that Arthur died, with Mordred, at the battle of Camlann; the dates of the battles are 516 (or 518) and 537 (or 539), respectively.

There has been much speculation about the exact location of Badon and Camlann.

KING ARTHUR'S TOMB
Slaughter Bridge

A mile or so north of Camelford is the tiny hamlet of Slaughter Bridge, just east of the old Camelford railway station which once served Victorian tourists destined for Tintagel. According to local tradition, the nearby water meadows were the site of the battle of Camlann in which King Arthur was mortally wounded and Mordred was killed. A short distance upstream from the medieval bridge is a moss-covered stone known as King Arthur's Tomb or Grave. It lies on the west bank of the River Camel and bears a sixth- or seventh-century inscription which reads *LATINI IC IACIT FILIUS MAGARI* or 'Latinus lies here, son of Magarus'. At one time it was believed, in error, that Arthur's name could be recognized in the inscription. The stone is nine and a half feet long and once marked a grave in the meadow: it was later used as a footbridge. The name Slaughter Bridge is thought to derive from a battle which took place nearby in the ninth century between the Saxons and Cornish. The River Camel rises on Hendraburnick Down and passes through Slaughter Bridge, Camelford and Wadebridge to enter the sea at Padstow.

Tradition places Camlann at Slaughter Bridge in Cornwall, but historians generally agree that the more likely location is near the Roman fort of Camboglanna (Castlesteads) in Cumbria. Among the possible sites for Badon are one of the hills overlooking Bath, Badbury Rings (a hillfort near Wimborne, Dorset) and Liddington Castle (formerly Badbury Castle, a hillfort south of Swindon, Wiltshire).

Geoffrey of Monmouth, who was branded 'the father of lies', included Arthur in his *Historia Regum Britanniae* (The History of the Kings of Britain), completed *c.* 1136. There are a number of theories regarding Geoffrey's original source, none of which can be substantiated, but all who have studied the evidence accept that it was based on an oral or written tradition and was not simply invented.

During the twelfth century the popularity of the Arthurian romances spread throughout Christendom. Appropriately, Arthur's grave was discovered at Glastonbury in 1191. Geoffrey exploited the fashion in his *Historia*, which poets like Wace and Layamon not only rendered into verse but translated from Latin into French and English respectively. The French poet Chrétien de Troyes introduced further elements, notably the chivalrous adventures of individual knights and mention of the Holy Grail. Among later writers, Sir Thomas Malory in *Le Morte d'Arthur* (completed *c.* 1469) and Alfred Tennyson in *Idylls of the King* (started in 1855) revived and added to the legend.

Over the centuries Arthur was transformed from a Dark Age warrior into a medieval king who held court at Camelot and was the leader of a chivalrous band of followers known as the Knights of the Round Table. Although the knights set out to seek adventure and to perform heroic deeds, their principal and avowed aim was the quest for the Holy Grail, the cup used by Christ at the Last Supper.

Today, names like Camelot, Merlin, Avalon, Excalibur, Lyonesse, Lancelot, Guinevere, Tristan and Isolde stir the imagination, conjuring up images of romance, magic and chivalry. Although Arthurian sites can be found throughout Britain, the greatest concentration lies in the West Country, particularly in Cornwall. They include Tintagel Castle, Arthur's legendary birthplace; Slaughter Bridge, traditional site of the battle of Camlann; Camelford, claimed by some to be Camelot; Dozmary Pool and Loe Pool, reputed alternatives for the lake in which Sir Bedivere begrudgingly cast Excalibur.

Whether Arthur was real or fictitious may never be proven, but for those, like Tennyson, who follow the 'gleam' of Arthurian legend the quest inevitably leads to Tintagel, to the wild granite peninsula of Cornwall and to the lost land of Lyonesse.

PARISH CHURCH
Morwenstow

Hidden amidst trees on the south side of a deep coombe, the mainly Norman church of Morwenstow is dedicated to St Morwenna and St John the Baptist. The eccentric poet-parson Robert Stephen Hawker, who founded the modern Harvest Festival, was vicar of the remote parish for forty-one years from 1834. It is reputed that his parishioners were 'a mixed multitude of smugglers, wreckers and dissenters'. With a coastline notorious for shipwrecks, Hawker felt that it was his duty to give a Christian burial to all the bodies washed up on the jagged rocks. The white figurehead in the churchyard marks the grave of the captain and crew of the Scottish brig *Caledonia*, which ran aground in 1842. The vicarage below the church was built by Hawker, who embellished it with chimneys said to resemble the church towers of places he had been associated with, apart from the kitchen chimney, which was shaped like his mother's tomb. Hawker's Hut, built of driftwood and sited on the edge of the cliffs overlooking the Atlantic, is one of the smallest properties owned by the National Trust. Here Hawker smoked opium, 'alone with his books, his thoughts and with God'.

COMPASS POINT
Bude

Once a small fishing port on the east bank of the River Neet, Bude began to develop into a holiday resort in the early nineteenth century. Today the area is popular with surfers, Crooklets Beach being known as 'Britain's Bondi'. On Efford Down, south of Bude Haven, the sandstone Storm Tower at Compass Point was built by Sir Thomas Dyke Acland in the 1830s. Each of the eight sides represents a point of the compass. The Bude Canal, constructed between 1819 and 1825, ran for some thirty-five miles, from the sea lock at Bude Haven to Druxton, near Launceston, with branches to Holsworthy and Alfardisworthy Reservoir. Built to transport large quantities of lime-rich sea sand inland for agricultural use, the waterway (noted for its wheeled 'tub-boats') closed in 1891 due to competition from the railways. The cliffs along the coast are unstable: composed of layers of sandstone and soft shale, they were formed on the bed of a sea about 300 million years ago and have been tilted from the horizontal to the vertical and through all angles between. Uneven erosion of the rock strata has created a succession of parallel reefs or ribs stretching out to sea.

ROCK CARVING
Rocky Valley

Beyond St Nectan's glen the Trevillett stream flows north-west through Rocky Valley to the Atlantic. Carved on a rock face behind the ruins of an ancient watermill are two small and rare traditional Cretan-type mazes, thought to date from the Early Bronze Age (1800–1400 BC). The people of the Bronze Age were immigrants from Europe with sufficient knowledge of metals to make tools and weapons. They buried their dead in round barrows, or tumuli, of which many hundreds can still be found dotted throughout the Cornish countryside. They also erected stone circles and menhirs (standing stones). The greatest concentrations of these, together with Bronze Age boundary walls, field systems and hut circles, survive on the moors of Bodmin and Dartmoor. Rocky Valley was once the haunt of the chough, now extinct in Cornwall. Legend says that King Arthur did not die at the battle of Camlann, that instead his soul was incarnated in the chough and that one day, like the bird, he will return. Another Arthurian legend says that the Round Table lies beneath nearby Bossiney Mound and rises from the earth in a flash of silver light on Midsummer's Eve.

TINTAGEL CASTLE

Long thought to have been the legendary birthplace of King Arthur, Tintagel Castle stands high on a rocky headland overlooking the Atlantic Ocean. Almost an island, it is connected to the mainland by a low and crumbling isthmus. Geoffrey of Monmouth said that access was 'so narrow that three armed soldiers could hold it against the whole kingdom of Britain'. Today the ruins of the castle are reached by a long, steep flight of steps and a wooden bridge. The castle was first built in the 1140s by Reginald, Earl of Cornwall, an illegitimate son of Henry I. It was altered and enlarged by Richard, Lord of Tintagel, in the middle of the thirteenth century. From 1337 the castle belonged to Edward the Black Prince, eldest son of Edward III. It eventually became a prison. During the sixteenth century the sea washed much of the narrow neck away and parts of the castle with it. Leland noted *c.*1540 that 'the buildings of the castle be sore weather-beaten and in ruin'. Today the property is in the care of English Heritage. The church of St Materiana stands in remote isolation on the cliff south of the castle. The Old Post Office in Tintagel is owned by the National Trust.

MERLIN'S CAVE
Tintagel

Some 270 feet beneath the black, jagged ruins of Tintagel Castle is a deep cavern, filled at high tide with the roar of the Atlantic Ocean. Tunnelling right through the base of the castle headland, the cave opens out on the other side onto a small beach of rounded pebbles and slate, where, according to tradition, the infant Arthur was washed ashore to be found by Merlin. The wizard, whose ghost is reputed to haunt the cave, gave the future king his name and arranged for the boy to be brought up secretly by Sir Ector and his wife. The earliest mention of Arthur's connection with the castle at Tintagel occurs in Geoffrey of Monmouth's twelfth-century *Historia Regum Britanniae.* According to Monmouth, it was through Merlin's potent magic that King Uther Pendragon was able to take on the appearance of Gorlois, Duke of Cornwall, and enter the castle. Once inside he made love to Gorlois' wife, Ygerna or Igraine, and Arthur was conceived. Cornwall is sometimes known as the Land of Merlin. During the eighteenth and nineteenth centuries small sailing vessels, laden with coal from South Wales, landed on the beach to unload their cargo and take on slate from the Glebe Cliff Quarries.

THE WATERFALL
St Nectan's Glen

According to legend, the eerie sound of ghostly, chanting monks can at certain times be heard in the thickly wooded glen between Tintagel and Boscastle. This dark, secluded valley takes its name from the sixth-century Welsh hermit St Nectan, who built a small chapel or hermitage on the banks of the River Trevillett. From a viewpoint on the top of the tower, it is said, he rang a silver bell to warn approaching ships of the danger of submerged rocks. He was killed by pagan robbers and, during the Middle Ages, his shrine at Hartland, North Devon, became a centre of pilgrimage. In 1860 a small cottage was erected on the site of the ruined hermitage, incorporating part of the chapel and possibly the foundations of the tower. Just below 'The Hermitage', which was extended in 1900, is St Nectan's (or St Knighton's) Kieve, a huge rock basin some twenty feet deep. There is a tradition that the saint was buried in the river bed below the kieve. A waterfall plummets some sixty feet into the kieve through a natural arch. The glen and waterfall are privately owned, and admission is only via the Hermitage Tea Gardens, where a fee is charged.

DOYDEN POINT
Portquin

The wild and rugged coast between Doyden Point and Pentire Point, owned by the National Trust, forms a four-mile stretch of the long-distance South West Coast Path. The battlemented folly on Doyden Point, at the mouth of the Portquin inlet, was built by Samuel Symons, a Wadebridge merchant, who bought the headland in 1827. It is now a National Trust holiday home. Portquin was once used for shipping locally mined lead and antimony and (like its neighbours, Port Isaac and Port Gaverne) for the export of Delabole slate. In 1861 records state that there were twenty-three houses and eighty inhabitants. Today, all that is left of the fishing village are the converted fish cellars and a few cottages, some of which are let as holiday homes by the National Trust. The clifftop Doyden House was built *c.* 1870 as a retirement home for a prison governor. Why the port was abandoned remains a mystery: some say that the men of the village were all lost at sea during a storm, others that they emigrated to Canada after several bad pilchard seasons. On the horizon in the photograph are the Rumps, part of the mainland, and Mouls Island.

ST ENODOC'S CHURCH
Trebetherick

St Enodoc's church, in the parish of St Minver, was dug out of the encroaching sands in 1863 and restored the following year. In the mistaken belief that it was sinking, it came to be affectionately known as 'Sinkininny' or 'Sinking Neddy'. An account dated 1919–21 notes that 'the sands had blown higher than the eastern gable, the wet came in freely, the high pews were mouldy-green and worm-eaten and bats flew about, living in the belfry'. The present church, now surrounded by a golf course, may have been built on the site of a cave used as a hermitage by St Enodoc, about whom very little is known. It is thought that he may have baptized his converts at the Jesus Well, near Rock, less than a mile distant. Parts of the church are Norman while the leaning spire dates from the thirteenth century. It is said that by ecclesiastical law the vicar had to enter the church at least once a year, and that when the church was almost completely buried in the sand entry was made through the roof. Sir John Betjeman and his mother are buried in the churchyard – the poet's grave is near the lych gate – and inside the church is a plaque in memory of his father.

PORT ISAAC

The remote fishing village of Port Isaac, with its close-packed cottages, narrow alleys or 'opes' and small harbour, lies at the bottom of a steep coombe five miles north of Wadebridge. Its name is thought to be derived from the Cornish 'porth', meaning cove or harbour, and 'ysek', meaning corn, suggesting that it may have been a port for the export of corn. By the end of the sixteenth century slate from the Delabole quarry, near Camelford, was being shipped from the port. As in many other coastal villages in Cornwall, the livelihood of the inhabitants was once dependent on fishing, particularly for pilchards. The first lifeboat station (later to become the post office) was established in 1869. The present inshore lifeboat, established in 1967, is housed in the fish cellars. The streets in the old village are notoriously narrow, some only seven feet wide, while Squeeze-ee-Belly Alley, the narrowest of the opes, is just over eighteen inches wide. The tiny five-sided house known as the Birdcage was built in the nineteenth century by Valentine Powell Richards.

JAMAICA INN
Bolventor

Immortalized in the novel by Daphne du Maurier, Jamaica Inn will always be associated with smugglers. Originally a coaching hostelry known as the New Inn, the much altered slate-hung building, with its Joss Merlyn's Museum Bar, Dame Daphne du Maurier Room and Potter's Museum of Curiosity, stands in the tiny hamlet of Bolventor, surrounded by the wild, brooding landscape of Bodmin Moor. Brown Willy, the highest point on the moor at 1375 feet above sea level, lies just over two miles north-west. Rising amidst the marshland to the east of Brown Willy is the source of the River Fowey; Bodmin Moor, covering an area of approximately 120 square miles, was originally called Fowey Moor. Just off the main moorland road between Bodmin and Altarnun, three miles south-west of Jamaica Inn, lies the tiny village of Temple, named after the Knights Templars who built a hospice there. Enjoying special privileges, the church acquired a reputation in the past as a Cornish Gretna Green, where couples could be married without reading the banns beforehand. As Richard Carew noted, 'Many a bad marriage bargain is there yearly slubbered up'.

LANHYDROCK HOUSE
near Bodmin

Considered by Pevsner to be one of the grandest houses in Cornwall 'and certainly the grandest of its century', Lanhydrock House lies amid extensive wooded parkland overlooking the valley of the River Fowey. Until the Dissolution of the Monasteries in 1539 the land was owned by the Augustinian Priory of St Mary and St Petroc, Bodmin. It was bought by Sir Richard Robartes, an affluent merchant and banker from Truro, in 1620. He died while the first house was being built, leaving his son John to complete it in 1635–42. Originally laid out around four sides of a quadrangle, the east wing was demolished *c.* 1780. In 1857 Thomas Agar-Robartes, later first Baron Robartes of Lanhydrock and Truro, remodelled and enlarged the house. Only the north wing, with its seventeenth-century gallery and plasterwork, and the detached gatehouse (completed 1651) survived the disastrous fire of 1881. It was rebuilt by the second Baron to the original plan, but incorporating the latest comforts and conveniences of the late Victorian era. The house, built of local granite, lies almost three miles south-east of Bodmin and is owned by the National Trust.

KING DONIERT'S STONE
St Cleer

Inside a small enclosure on the south side of the Redgate to Darite road, north-west of St Cleer, are two stones, both decorated with interlaced carving. On one is inscribed *DONIERT ROGAVIT PRO ANIMA*, which may be translated 'Doniert ordered [this cross] for [the good of] his soul'. Doniert is thought to be Durngarth or Dwngarth, King of Cornwall, who was drowned in about AD 875 (according to the Welsh *Brut y Tywysogyon* or Chronicle of the Princes). Both stones, which have mortises and originally supported cross heads, are in the care of English Heritage. Not far from the church of St Cleer is a holy well, the water from which was once reputed to cure madness. Richard Carew notes in his *Survey of Cornwall* that in the late sixteenth century there were many 'boussening' or ducking-wells in Cornwall for 'curing of mad men'. The 'frantic person' would be knocked into the water, where he would be tossed 'up and down, alongst and athwart the water, until the patient, by foregoing his strength, had somewhat forgot his fury. Then was he conveyed to the Church and certain Masses sung over him.' If he hadn't recovered 'he was boussened again and again, while there remained in him any hope of life, for recovery'.

DOZMARY POOL
Bodmin Moor

After the battle of Camlann, according to Malory, the grievously wounded King Arthur ordered Sir Bedivere to cast Excalibur into the lake. Unable to throw the precious sword away, Bedivere hid it instead. When asked by Arthur what he had seen, Bedivere replied that he had seen nothing but 'waves and winds'. Arthur knew that he was lying and commanded Bedivere to go back and do as he had been told. Once more Bedivere returned without having obeyed. Again Arthur asked him what he had seen. 'I saw nothing but the waters wap and waves wan', said the knight. The third time Bedivere reluctantly threw the sword into the lake and it was caught by a hand before being drawn under. Bedivere then carried the king to the water's edge, where a barge bore him to Avilion (Avalon). Among the sites reputed to have received Excalibur is Dozmary Pool on Bodmin Moor. Said to be bottomless, the pool dried up in 1859 and was found to be relatively shallow. It is also associated with the wicked John Tregeagle (see p. 48), who, by way of punishment, was set the impossible task of emptying the pool with a leaky limpet shell.

STOWE'S HILL
Bodmin Moor

Crowning the summit of Stowe's Hill (1250 feet), on the south-eastern edge of Bodmin Moor, are a number of natural weather-worn granite tors, the most famous of which is the Cheesewring (not shown in the photograph). This 'wonderful pile of rocks', as Thomas Staniforth wrote in 1800, now stands on the very edge of a disused granite quarry. Also on Stowe's Hill is Stowe's Pound, a prehistoric enclosure thought to date from the Bronze Age. During the eighteenth century Daniel Gumb, an eccentric stonecutter with a passion for mathematics and astronomy, lived with his wife and children in a nearby cave, which bears his name and the date 1735. Locally known as the 'Mountain Philosopher', he scored the roof with 'diagrams illustrative of some of the most difficult problems of Euclid' (*Murray's Handbook*, 1859). Quarrying caused the original cave to collapse but it has been rebuilt with granite blocks. In the churchyard of St Melor, Linkinhorne, Gumb cut several gravestones, one, dated 1742 and 1744, bears an epitaph for two women: 'Here we lye without the wall; / 'Twas full within they made a brawl, / Here we lye no rent to pay, / And yet we lye so warm as they.' He died in 1776.

THE HURLERS
Minions

On the south-eastern margin of Bodmin Moor, near Minions village, are the remains of three Bronze Age stone circles known as the Hurlers. Close together, they are roughly aligned in a north-east to south-west direction. Excavation has revealed that the central circle was paved with granite slabs and connected to the northern circle by a stone path. From north to south, the circles are approximately 114 feet, 140 feet and 108 feet in diameter respectively. The southern circle is the most ruinous. Legend says that they are named after a group of Cornish hurlers, who insisted on playing the game on the Sabbath and, as punishment, were turned to stone. The two upright menhirs nearby are said to be two players who tried, but failed, to escape. To the north-east of the circles is the Rillaton Bronze Age barrow, which yielded a unique corrugated gold cup thought to have come from Mycenae in Greece. In addition to prehistoric remains, the area bears evidence of past tin- and copper-mining activity. The engine house in the photograph was built in 1881 and restored in 1991.

TRETHEVY QUOIT
Tremar

Trethevy Quoit is a Penwith chamber tomb, consisting of six stones, one of which is a dividing slab, surmounted by a massive capstone. It stands between the villages of Tremar and Darite, some three miles north of Liskeard. The capstone, almost fourteen feet long, leans at a precarious angle due to the collapse into the chamber of the western support stone. Towering over fourteen feet at its highest point, the capstone is inexplicably pierced by a fist-sized hole in one corner. Restricted access into the chamber can be gained by a rectangular 'porthole' cut out of a corner of the dividing slab. Originally covered by a large mound of earth, the Neolithic burial chamber is thought to be over 4000 years old. Tombs such as this were constructed for collective and successive burials, similar to family vaults, each chamber containing perhaps twenty or more carefully laid-out bodies. In some cases excavation has revealed that the remains of earlier burials have been cleared aside to make room for later ones. After four millennia, however, evidence is scant: the bones have usually been eaten away by the acid soils of the region, while grave goods have long since been removed.

CHURCH OF ST GERMANUS
St Germans

St Germanus, Bishop of Auxerre in France, visited Cornwall in the fifth century, founding a Celtic church and monastery on a ridge above the River Tiddy, nine miles south-east of Liskeard. Named after him, St Germans – although now a small village – became an important borough town. In about 926 Athelstan, King of Wessex, created a Cornish diocese with St Germans as its seat, making the Anglo-Saxon church the first cathedral in Cornwall. On the death of Bishop Burhwold in 1043 the see passed to his nephew, already Bishop of Crediton. In 1050 Bishop Leofric moved the seat of the united sees of Cornwall and Devon to Exeter. Cornwall did not have its own diocese again until 1876, when the bishopric of Truro was established. In about 1180 Bishop Bartholomew converted Leofric's college of secular canons into a priory of Augustinian canons, the new church finally being consecrated in 1261. Despite the Dissolution, much of this Norman church remains, including the magnificent west doorway. In 1563 the priory was acquired by the Eliots (later Earls of St Germans) who incorporated parts of the building into their family seat, Port Eliot.

RAME HEAD

Rame Head, the cone-shaped headland at the western entrance to Plymouth Sound, is topped by the ruins of a medieval chapel dedicated to St Michael. It also supports the earthwork remains of an Iron Age fort. The church in the tiny hamlet of Rame dates from Norman times and the slate tower with its broached spire is a notable landmark. To the west are the sweeping sands of Whitsand Bay, where numerous ships have been driven ashore while trying to round Rame Head in a gale. Eight miles south of the headland is the Eddystone reef, the scene of so many wrecks that it was decided to erect a lighthouse there – the first ever to be built on a wave-swept rock. Henry Winstanley erected the first one on the site in 1698; it was rebuilt the following year, and he lost his life, with others, when the replacement was swept away during a storm in 1703. The present, and fifth, lighthouse to be built on the rock was designed by James Douglass and completed in 1882. To the east of Rame Head, around Penlee Point, are the old fishing villages of Cawsand and Kingsand and, beyond, Mount Edgcumbe Country Park with 800 acres of parkland, gardens and woodland overlooking Plymouth, Drake's Island and the Sound.

Plymouth and South-Western Devon

BUCKLAND ABBEY
Buckland Monachorum

Buckland Abbey, eight miles north of Plymouth, was founded in 1273 by Amicia, Countess of Devon, as a monastery for Cistercian monks. In 1541, after the Dissolution, it was bought by Sir Richard Grenville, who installed his son Roger in the property. Roger was drowned in 1545 when the *Mary Rose* sank off Portsmouth, and Buckland passed to his son and heir, Richard Grenville (1542–91), soldier and adventurer, who also became a knight. In 1585 Grenville attempted to found a settlement on Roanoke Island, Virginia (now in North Carolina), and in 1591 was in command of the *Revenge* when it was captured by the Spanish after an epic fight off the Azores, an exploit commemorated in Tennyson's poem 'The Revenge'. Grenville died of his wounds a few days later. Buckland, which Grenville had converted into a private house, was bought by Sir Francis Drake in 1582, the year he became Mayor of Plymouth. The Drake Gallery contains the drum, said to beat if England is ever in danger, which is immortalized in the nautical ballad 'Drake's Drum' (1897) by Sir Henry Newbolt. The house and gardens are open to the public.

Originally a fishing village called Sutton, the city of Plymouth lies between the estuaries of the River Plym (Cattewater) and the River Tamar (Hamoaze). Plymouth Sound, formed where the Cattewater and Hamoaze meet, is one of the finest natural deepwater anchorages in Britain. Sutton Harbour (and the Cattewater) was the port's main harbour until the establishment of the naval dockyard at Devonport on the Hamoaze in 1691. It was from the old harbour during Elizabethan times that almost every major expedition of discovery, colonization and commercial venture departed. Among those who sailed from the port were Drake, Hawkins and Raleigh, all Devonians, all privateers.

Francis Drake, who was born near Tavistock *c*. 1540, set sail from Plymouth in the *Pelican* (renamed the *Golden Hind*) in 1577 and successfully circumnavigated the world. Landing on the coast of present-day California, he claimed the land for the Queen, naming it 'Nova Albion'. In April 1581, just six months after his return to Plymouth, he was knighted. While playing a game of bowls on Plymouth Hoe in 1588 he received news that the Spanish Armada had been sighted in the English Channel. Waiting until the tide had ebbed, he set sail – serving as vice-admiral under Lord Admiral Charles Howard of Effingham – with the much smaller but faster English fleet. After a running battle the Spanish were finally defeated at Calais, and Drake became a national hero. He purchased Buckland Abbey from Sir Richard Grenville in 1581, became Mayor of Plymouth in 1582 and a Member of Parliament in 1584. He died on 28 January 1596 during a voyage to the West Indies and was buried at sea.

Drake's cousin, Sir John Hawkins, who died on board ship in 1595 on the same West Indies voyage, was born at Plymouth in 1532. He embarked on his first slave-trading expedition in 1562 on behalf of a syndicate of London merchants. The venture proved to be so profitable that he was able to raise the finance for a second voyage in 1564 from such eminent people as Robert Dudley (later Earl of Leicester) and Queen Elizabeth herself. His third expedition, in 1567, on which he was accompanied by Drake, ended in disaster. While the six English ships were harboured at San Juan de Ulua, near Veracruz, Mexico, they were attacked by a Spanish fleet. Only the two ships commanded by Hawkins and Drake managed to make the voyage back to England. Hawkins became Treasurer of the Navy in 1577 and began to rebuild the fleet with swifter, more manoeuvrable, more heavily armed galleons. It was this new, more efficient navy that managed to defeat the Armada in 1588. Hawkins, serving as rear-admiral, was third in command and was knighted on the deck of the Ark Royal.

Sir Walter Raleigh, courtier, explorer, historian, poet and colonizer, was born *c.* 1552 at Hayes Barton, near East Buddleigh. He was brought to the attention of the Queen by the Earl of Leicester and through her favour his fortunes changed dramatically. He became a knight, Lord Warden of the Stannaries (in control of mining in Cornwall and Devon), Lord-Lieutenant of Cornwall, Vice-Admiral of the West and Captain of the Guard. He also became a Member of Parliament for Devon in 1584. In that same year, having been granted a patent to found a colony, he equipped an expedition to explore the Atlantic coast of North America for a suitable settlement site. Forbidden by the Queen to sail with the colonists himself, he put his cousin, Sir Richard Grenville, in command of the fleet of seven ships which set off from Plymouth in April 1585. They left over one hundred settlers on Roanoke Island and returned home, where they reported their findings to Raleigh, who christened the new territory Virginia in honour of the Virgin Queen. When Grenville returned with supplies the following year he found that all the survivors of the colony had gone back to England with Drake, who had called at the settlement on his way home from the West Indies. Raleigh, however, was not to be deterred. A second colony was established on Roanoke Island in 1587, but three years later the settlers had disappeared. After losing the Queen's favour by secretly marrying, Raleigh embarked on numerous expeditions across the Atlantic. When the Queen died in 1603 he was stripped of his offices and estates and imprisoned in the Tower for treason. He was released, but not pardoned, in 1616 and two years later, after a fruitless expedition to find Eldorado (during which his son was killed), he was executed.

Among other noted Elizabethan seamen associated with Plymouth are Sir Martin Frobisher (*c.* 1535–94), who sailed in search of the North-West Passage in 1576 and discovered Frobisher Bay, and Sir Humphrey Gilbert (*c.* 1539–83), 'Father of British Colonization', who sailed from Plymouth in 1583 and claimed Newfoundland for the Queen, but went down with his ship on the homeward voyage.

PLYMOUTH HOE

Plymouth Hoe, the historic limestone headland overlooking the Sound, is the site of various memorials and monuments including Drake's statue (unveiled by Lady Elliot Drake in 1884) and the Armada memorial (unveiled by HRH the Duke of Edinburgh in 1890). Smeaton's Tower, built in 1759 by John Smeaton, originally stood on the Eddystone reef, fourteen miles out to sea. Replaced by a larger lighthouse in 1882, it was dismantled stone by stone and re-erected on the Hoe. The Royal Citadel, erected in 1666, was originally next to the Elizabethan fort, built to defend the town and harbour from attack by sea. Fort and citadel were eventually joined. The *Mayflower*, carrying the Pilgrim Fathers to the New World, set sail from Plymouth in September 1620, reaching the North American coast in November. The settlement they established in Massachusetts was appropriately named New Plymouth. A list of the fifty-two passengers hangs on a large board on the wall of Island House, at the entrance to New Street on the Barbican, where some of the Pilgrims were reputedly entertained before leaving for America.

NOSS MAYO
from Newton Ferrers

'The Yealm Estuary', states *Murray's Handbook* of 1859, 'although seldom visited, is rich in the picturesque. The water is transparent, the course of the inlet tortuous, and the hills which enclose it heathery or wooded, and fringed at their bases by a margin of rocks.' Facing each other across a creek of the River Yealm are the twin villages of Newton Ferrers and Noss Mayo, the former recorded in the *Domesday Book* as 'Niwetone' and in 1303 as 'Neweton Ferers' after the de Ferrers family who once owned the manor. In 1286 a market was established at Noss Mayo and in the fourteenth century it became a minor borough. Today it is a small fishing village. The sheltered creek between the villages is a popular mooring for yachts and small boats. On the edge of the cliff overlooking Stoke Bay, just over a mile south-east of Noss Mayo, is the ruined but partly restored church of St Peter the Poor Fisherman, Revelstoke. Thought to date from the fourteenth century, the chapel was badly damaged by a storm in 1840, declared unsafe in 1869 and finally abandoned in 1882 when the lord of the manor, Edward Charles Baring, Lord Revelstoke, built a new church at Noss Mayo, also dedicated to St Peter.

BURGH ISLAND
Bigbury Bay

At low tide it is possible to walk, via an isthmus of firm sand, across the estuary of the River Avon to Burgh Island, opposite Bigbury-on-Sea. When the tide is in, a unique 'sea tractor' (shown in the picture), specially built for the purpose, ferries visitors the 300 yards to and from the island. Weighing ten tons, it will operate in seven feet of water, though breakdowns have occurred, notably in 1971 when the passengers had to be rescued by boat. Originally known as St Michael's after a medieval chapel which once stood on the top, the island became 'la Burgh', meaning stronghold, in the fifteenth century, later 'Burrow' or 'Burrough' and eventually 'Burgh'. William Camden wrote, 'Where Avon's waters with the sea are mixt, St Michael firmly on a rock is fixt'. Today the remains of a huer's hut crowns the summit, a reminder that fishing for pilchards using seine nets once took place in the bay. The Pilchard Inn, dated 1336, was a smugglers' haunt. The hotel was built by Archibald Nettlefold in 1929 and, after staying there, Agatha Christie was inspired to write *Ten Little Niggers* or *And Then There Were None* (1939) and *Evil under the Sun* (1941).

SALCOMBE
from Sharpitor

A popular haven for yachtsmen, with a sheltered natural harbour leading to a wealth of tidal creeks, Salcombe lies on the hilly west bank of the Kingsbridge estuary (more exactly a 'ria', or drowned valley, rather than an estuary). Leland described it as a 'fisher town' *c.* 1540, but during medieval times the main settlement at the mouth of the estuary had been East Portlemouth, opposite. Salcombe developed as a shipbuilding town, renowned for its fast schooners, which were able to bring fruit in good condition from the West Indies, the Azores and the Mediterranean. It became a retirement and holiday resort during the early nineteenth century, and held its first annual regatta in 1857. The remains of one of Henry VIII's castles, known as Fort Charles, can be seen at the southern end of the harbour. In 1646, during the Civil War, it was besieged for four months by the Parliamentarians. Sharpitor House, set in six acres of sub-tropical gardens and owned by the National Trust, houses the Overbeck Museum of local bygones. The old market town and former inland port of Kingsbridge stands at the head of the estuary.

START POINT

The distinctive ridged headland of Start Point is composed of mica schist, an ancient rock which runs in an east-west band from Bolt Head to Start Point and is found nowhere else in Devon. 'The ridge', according to *Murray's Handbook*, 'stretches boldly to sea, sloped on each side like the roof of a house, and crowned along its entire length by fanciful crags, strangely weathered, and shaggy with moss'. 'Start' is derived from the Old English 'steort', meaning tail. The lighthouse, established in 1836, warns shipping of the Blackstone Rock and the Skerries shingle bank in Start Bay. These, coupled with dangerous currents, have claimed many ships over the years. In one storm alone, in March 1891, five vessels were lost. Not only ships but whole villages, including Hallsands and Strete-Undercliffe, have been destroyed by the ferocity of the sea along this part of the coast. In medieval times the headland was used as a gallows site. The coast between Start Point and Slapton Ley is on a major route for birds crossing the Channel from the Continent and attracts many summer and winter migrants. Prawle Point, a few miles to the south-west, is the most southerly tip of Devon.

HALLSANDS

During a severe storm on 26 January 1917 almost all the houses in the fishing village of Hallsands were washed away. It was the last of a succession of storms that had gradually destroyed the village, which, in the 1850s, had had at least thirty-seven houses and 128 inhabitants. Standing almost in a line along a rocky ledge, the houses were originally protected from the sea by a substantial shingle beach. Between 1897 and 1902, however, extensive dredging offshore for shingle to extend the Devonport dockyard at Plymouth is thought to have caused a dramatic fall in the level of the beach, removing the village's natural sea defences. A sea wall was built by Richard Hansford Worth in 1903–4, but it proved ineffective against the easterly gale of 1917 which left only one house standing and the rest irreparably damaged. The villagers, who all managed to escape with their lives, found themselves not only homeless but destitute. Although they were eventually awarded compensation, it was not enough to rebuild the village and they were forced to abandon it.

SLAPTON LEY

The largest natural freshwater lake in Devon, Slapton Ley is separated from the sea by a shingle ridge two-and-a-half miles long, which was formed by glacial meltwaters after the last Ice Age. Experts believe that the 445-acre lake, only nine feet at its deepest, was established by about 1000 years ago. Designated a Site of Special Scientific Interest, the Ley is an important nature reserve, owned by the Herbert Whitley Trust and managed by the Slapton Ley Field Centre in Slapton village. Divided into the Higher and Lower Ley by the road which leads from the ridge to the village, the lake – rich in plant and animal life – is visited by many rare migratory birds. The shingle beach at Slapton Sands was used by the Americans for beach landing practice prior to the assault on Normandy in June 1944. A granite monument by the roadside acknowledges the 'generosity of local people who left their homes and lands' to enable the rehearsal to take place. The village of Torcross, standing at the southern end of the Ley, was almost destroyed by storms in 1951 and 1979. The present sea wall was built in 1980.

DARTMOUTH AND KINGSWEAR CASTLES
Dartmouth

Guarding the deep-water, sheltered anchorage at the mouth of the River Dart are two forts, part of a chain of sea defences erected to defend the English coast from French and Breton raiders: Dartmouth Castle (in the foreground), built in 1481–94 and noted for being the first in Britain to be designed with gun ports for heavy artillery, and Kingswear Castle (in the background), started in 1491 and later converted into a private residence. Dartmouth, which superseded Totnes in medieval times as the major port on the Dart, was used as an assembly point for English ships leaving on the Second and Third Crusades in 1147 and 1190 respectively. It prospered on the export of Devon cloth and the import of French wine and, later, on the exploitation of fish from the North Atlantic. The ancient town grew up around the harbour and contains many buildings of interest, the oldest being the Cherub, in Higher Street, dating from the fourteenth century. The Butterwalk, fronting the Quay, dates from 1628–40. The Britannia Royal Naval College, on a commanding hilltop site to the north, was built by Sir Aston Webb in 1902–5. Thomas Newcomen, who invented the first atmospheric steam engine, was born in the town in 1663.

BRIXHAM

Devon's foremost fishing port until it was superseded by Plymouth in the 1870s, Brixham lies at the southern end of Tor Bay, overlooking Paignton and Torquay. The port is noted for the development, towards the end of the eighteenth century, of the Brixham trawler, for its size one of the most powerful sailing vessels ever built. The few sailing trawlers that remain of the once great fleet are used as yachts. Permanently moored in the harbour is a full-size replica of Drake's *Golden Hind*, which is open to the public. The Old Market House nearby, built in 1799, now contains a Tourist Information Centre and the British Fisheries Museum, which is devoted to the history of the industry. Although primarily catering for the holiday trade, the town still maintains a fishing fleet. On the quay is a statue of William, Prince of Orange, commemorating his unopposed landing at Brixham on 5 November 1688 with an army of around 10,000 men. When James II fled to France William became king of England. His promise is recorded: 'The liberties of England and the Protestant religion I will maintain.'

MARINA
Torquay

The largest resort in Devon, standing on a hilly site overlooking the harbour and Tor Bay, Torquay was a small fishing village until the beginning of the French wars in 1793, when the British navy anchored for long periods in the bay and used 'Torre Quay' as a supply base. Naval officers and their families, attracted by the mild winter climate, began to settle around the harbour. The wealthy, prevented from travelling abroad because of the wars, also visited the town and, with the fashion for sea bathing, Torquay was developed as a planned resort. Today, enhancing its almost Mediterranean air, Torquay sports sub-tropical vegetation and colourful gardens. The oldest building in the town is Torre Abbey, founded in 1196 by William de Brewer for Premonstratensian canons. After the Dissolution part of the ruined abbey was converted into a private residence. Owned by the Cary family since the Restoration, the house (remodelled in the Georgian style between 1700 and 1750) was bought by the town in 1930. It has numerous attractions and exhibitions, including an Agatha Christie memorial room. The house and grounds are open to the public.

OLDWAY MANSION
Paignton

Originally built in 1875 by George Bridgman for Isaac Singer, the sewing machine millionaire, and called by him 'the Wigwam', Oldway Mansion was remodelled in 1904–7 by his son, Paris Singer, partly in the style of the Palace of Versailles, with over 100 rooms, a Hall of Mirrors, a gallery, a marbled staircase and richly painted ceilings. The mansion is now owned by the Borough of Torbay, and the gardens and part of the house are open to the public. Kirkham House, nearby, is a late fourteenth- or early fifteenth-century town house, possibly built for an official of the Bishop of Exeter's palace. In the care of English Heritage and much restored, it too is open to the public. Coverdale Tower, near St John's church, which is all that remains of the Bishop's palace, is named after Miles Coverdale, translator of the Bible into English and Bishop of Exeter from 1551 to 1553. Paignton – one of the three Torbay 'English Riviera' towns – developed as a seaside resort in the early nineteenth century, with rapid expansion after the arrival of the railway from Exeter in 1859. The town's attractions include sandy beaches, a small harbour, a pleasure pier and Devon's largest zoological and botanical gardens.

BERRY POMEROY CASTLE

On a steep, wooded hillside overlooking the valley of Gatcombe Brook, three miles north-east of Totnes, are the ruins of Berry Pomeroy Castle, which date mainly from the fifteenth century. In about 1090, after the Norman Conquest, the Berry estate came into the possession of Ralf de Pomeroy and remained with the family until 1547, when it was bought by Edward Seymour, first Duke of Somerset and brother of Jane Seymour, third wife of Henry VIII. Somerset, who became Protector of the Realm to his nephew Edward VI, was executed in 1552. The castle, still owned by one of his descendants, is in the care of English Heritage. A substantial house stood on the site by the end of the thirteenth century but this was largely demolished to make room for the present fortified mansion, which was probably started *c.* 1460, when the gatehouse, curtain wall, Margaret Tower and Tower House (shown in the photograph) were built. The next major rebuilding programme, embodying advanced Renaissance architectural ideas which first appeared in England in the 1540s, was begun by Somerset *c.* 1548. He planned a vast new mansion, but only the north wing was ever completed. The castle was abandoned *c.* 1690.

FORGE AND WEAVER'S COTTAGE
Cockington

Preserved amidst the urban sprawl of Paignton and Torquay, the idyllic ancient village of Cockington has an abundance of thatched cottages, the oldest reputedly dating back to the eleventh century. The Weaver's Cottage, formerly part of the Home Farm, is said to be Anglo-Saxon in origin and may have been the home of the 'hind', or steward, of Alric – who is mentioned in the *Domesday Book* as owning the manor during the reign of Edward the Confessor (1042–66). Since 1939 the building has been used by John Mills & Sons, traditional handloom weavers from Scotland. The adjacent studio, once a granary, was destroyed by fire in 1968 and rebuilt. Cockington Forge, opposite, is said to date from the fourteenth century. It ceased working with the departure of the last blacksmith in 1971. The thatched Drum Inn, on the site of the old Church Inn, was designed by Edwin Lutyens and opened in 1936. Higher Lodge, at the entrance to the park, is thought to have been built in 1410. It was damaged by fire *c.* 1710 and rebuilt with tree trunks supporting the projecting upper floor. The park, which includes Cockington Court, is now in the care of the Borough of Torbay.

Lydford and Dartmoor

TAVISTOCK
from Whitchurch Common

Just outside the western boundary of the National Park, the ancient market town of Tavistock straddles the River Tavy, from which it takes the first part of its name. The latter part is derived from the Old English 'stoc', referring to the original small Anglo-Saxon settlement. It grew up around the Benedictine Abbey, founded in the tenth century, and Henry I granted the town its first market charter in the early twelfth century. Due to the boom in Dartmoor tin, it was made a 'stannary' or coinage town in 1281 – one of four in Devon. It became an important centre for the wool and cloth trade and from *c*. 1790 to 1870 it also prospered from copper mining. After the Dissolution the abbey and town became the property of the Russells, later Dukes of Bedford. The seventh Duke rebuilt the town centre in the nineteenth century, using the local grey-green Hurdwick stone. The present parish church of St Eustachius dates back to the early fourteenth century but it was largely rebuilt in the fifteenth. A statue of Sir Francis Drake, who was born at nearby Crowndale *c*. 1540, stands at the end of Plymouth Road.

Lydford, which lies just within the north-western boundary of the Dartmoor National Park, is thought to date back to Celtic times. Strategically situated on a natural promontory formed by the valleys of the River Lyd and a tributary stream, it became one of a series of fortified strongholds, or 'burhs', built during the reign of Alfred the Great (871–99) to defend the borders of the kingdom of Wessex against Danish attack. Its streets were laid out on a grid pattern and it was protected by massive earth ramparts, although in 997 – together with Tavistock – it was burned and looted by the Danes. Lydford remained an important military centre, however, and one of the principal towns in Devon, even possessing the right to mint its own coins from locally mined silver in the tenth and eleventh centuries.

After the Conquest, the Normans erected a fortress west of the church. The present castle, north-east of the church, was first built on level ground in 1195. The great keep was heightened and encircled by a ditch in the thirteenth century. Its prime use was as a court house and prison, particularly for those caught infringing the severe Forest and Stannary Laws, which protected the Crown's hunting and mineral rights on Dartmoor. A man found guilty of adulterating tin, for example, had three spoonfuls of the molten metal poured down his throat. It was said that by 'Lydford law' men were hanged first and tried afterwards. As a prison the castle gained a terrible reputation. In 1510 it was described as 'one of the most annoyous, contagious and detestable places within this realm'.

In 1239 the 'Forest' of Dartmoor was granted to Richard, Earl of Cornwall. Records state that it lay wholly within the parish of Lydford. The bounds of the forest were defined in 1240 (mainly using natural features) by the 'perambulation' of 'twelve loyal knights'. The 'waste' moor within the twenty-two parishes bordering on the forest boundaries was known as the 'Commons of Devonshire'. The term 'forest' meant not that the moor was covered with trees but that it was a royal hunting preserve, or 'chase'. Until 1204, when the people of Devon successfully petitioned King John to free large areas of land from the forest laws, all of the county was a royal forest. The king's charter of 'disafforestation', however, excluded Dartmoor and Exmoor.

The fact that Lydford was such a large parish, covering an area of seventy-eight square miles and stretching over the greater part of Dartmoor, caused much hardship for parishioners living on the other side of the forest. It meant, for example, that the dead had to be carried across the moor to Lydford church for burial. One of the ancient tracks is still known as the 'Lich Way', meaning the 'way of the corpse'.

One story tells of a traveller caught in the snow on Dartmoor who found refuge at an isolated farm. During the night he woke shivering and his attention was drawn to a large chest in the corner of the room, which he felt compelled to open. To his horror he found that it contained a corpse preserved in salt. The two-week-old body was, it turned out, 'only fayther' who, because of the snow, couldn't be taken to the church for burial and had been 'salted in'.

In his *Guide to Dartmoor* of 1912 William Crossing writes: 'When the moor was in a suitable condition, and the streams not in flood, the forest settlers journeyed to Lydford over the green paths that led them there direct; when the state of the weather rendered these routes difficult to follow a more circuitous one was chosen.'

In 1260 the inhabitants of Babeny and Pizwell (both on the Walla Brook near Bellever) successfully petitioned Bishop Walter Branscombe to allow them to attend Widecombe church instead of travelling the extra 'eight miles in fine weather and fifteen in foul' to Lydford.

Since 1337, when 'the Castle and Manor of Lydford, and the Chase of Dartmoor' were granted to Edward the Black Prince, the Forest of Dartmoor has belonged to the Duchy of Cornwall. The area, including the Commons of Devonshire, covers around 200 square miles.

Today the duchy owns almost a third of the Dartmoor National Park (designated in 1951), including the Military Training Areas (leased to the Ministry of Defence) and Dartmoor Prison at Princetown (leased to the Home Office). With the creation in the 1780s of the settlement of 'Prince's Town', Lydford lost the last vestige of its former importance. The Stannary and Duchy Courts were moved to the new town (in 1800 and 1828 respectively) and the castle at Lydford fell into decay. The present village, retaining one of the largest parishes in Devon, occupies a small part of the ancient town's defences.

LYDFORD CASTLE

Although now a small village, Lydford was once an important Anglo-Saxon town with a royal mint, producing silver coins known as 'Lydford Pennies'. Standing on a natural promontory above the wooded valleys of two streams, the settlement – with streets laid out on a grid pattern – is surrounded by the remains of defensive earthworks enclosing about twenty acres. The present castle was built in 1195, replacing an earlier Norman fortress west of the church. As a stannary prison it gained a cruel reputation. William Browne wrote in the early seventeenth century: 'I oft have heard of Lydford Law / How in the morn they hang and draw / and sit in judgement after.' South-west of the castle, near the entrance porch of the church of St Petrock, built on the site of an oratory (possibly Celtic), is the tomb of George Routleigh, watchmaker, who died in 1802 at the age of fifty-seven. The long inscription compares his life to the workings of a watch: '. . . Integrity was the main-spring, / And prudence the regulator / Of all the actions of his life. / Humane, generous, and liberal, / His hand never stopped / Till he had relieved distress. . . .' The parish is the largest in Devon.

ST MARY'S ABBEY
Buckfast

Prominently sited in the valley of the River Dart, two miles south-west of Ashburton, Buckfast Abbey was first founded in 1018 by King Canute, or Cnut, as a monastery for Benedictine monks. King Stephen refounded it as an abbey for Savigniac monks in 1136 and in 1147 (when the Savigniac and Cistercian orders were united) it became a Cistercian house. After the Dissolution in 1539 most of the buildings were destroyed or left to fall into ruin. In the early nineteenth century a small mansion was built on the site, using stone from the remaining walls. The mansion and what remained of the abbey were bought by an exiled community of French Benedictine monks in 1882. Dom Anscar Vonier, who became abbot of Buckfast in 1906 at the age of thirty, decided to rebuild the abbey in memory of his predecessor, Abbot Boniface Natter (1902–6). He had one experienced mason, Brother Peter, but no money. However, in January 1907, after an appeal for funds, work began with a small team of monks (never more than six). The Abbey Church was consecrated in 1932 and the tower completed in 1938. Shortly afterwards Abbot Vonier died, his work done. Visitors are always welcome.

LADY EXMOUTH FALLS
Canonteign

The estate at Canonteign, at the eastern extremity of the National Park, north-west of Chudleigh, was bought by Lady Pellew in 1812 while her husband, Sir Edward Pellew, a naval captain, was away at sea. In 1814 he became Lord Exmouth of Canonteign and two years later, after a successful campaign in Algiers (in which the dey was defeated and around a thousand Christian slaves freed), he retired and was given the title of Viscount. Although he did not live at Canonteign, his son Pownoll completed the present house and the family have lived here ever since. In 1880 the third Lady Exmouth created the waterfall named after her, diverting the mill leat of the abandoned Frank Mills lead and silver mine over the head of the Canonteign gorge. With a dramatic drop of 220 feet, it is advertised as 'England's highest waterfall'. Buzzard's View, at the top of the fall, offers a spectacular view over the surrounding countryside. The tenth Viscount Exmouth opened Canonteign Falls and Country Park to the public in 1985. His attractions include nature trails, lakeside picnic areas, the Bonehill Collection of Antique Farm Machinery, gift shops and a licensed restaurant.

WIDECOMBE-IN-THE-MOOR

Sheltering in the valley of the East Webburn River, six miles west of Bovey Tracey, Widecombe-in-the-Moor was an important tin-mining centre in the fifteenth and sixteenth centuries. It was during this period of prosperity that the 120-foot pinnacled and battlemented tower was added to the fourteenth-century church, which is sometimes called 'the Cathedral of the Moor'. The tall granite tower was struck by lightning during a service held on Sunday 21 October 1638. Part of the tower fell through the roof and a fireball passed through the church, killing four people and injuring a great many more. A poem describing the event – written by Richard Hill, the village schoolmaster – hangs on painted boards inside the tower. The village is famed for its annual fair, immortalized in the song 'Widdicombe Fair' (first published in 1880). The fair is still held on the second Tuesday in September. The Church House, built about 1500, was considered by Pevsner to be 'the grandest in the county, two-storeyed, all of granite ashlar'. It is owned by the National Trust.

BUCKLAND-IN-THE-MOOR

The tiny village of Buckland-in-the-Moor, surrounded by woodland, lies on the slopes of a small valley formed by the Ruddycleave Water, a tributary of the River Dart. At the point where the stream passes under the Ashburton road there are several thatched stone cottages, one of which is named after the water. At the top of the hill, overlooking the wooded valley of the River Webburn and Holne Chase, is the moorstone church of St Peter, which dates from the twelfth century but was rebuilt in the Perpendicular style in the late fifteenth century. Instead of numerals the clock face has letters reading 'MY DEAR MOTHER'. The memorial was put there in the late 1920s by the local landowner, William Whitley. He was also responsible for 'The Ten Commandments Stone' on Buckland Beacon (1281 feet above sea level). The 'stone' – two granite slabs, in fact – was inscribed in 1928 by an Exeter mason to mark Parliament's decision not to revise the Book of Common Prayer. Charles Kingsley was born in the vicarage at Holne, a few miles south, in 1819. He is commemorated in the north window of Holne church, installed in 1894.

HOUND TOR
Manaton

The huge, fractured granite outcrop of Hound Tor, near Manaton, is said to resemble a pack of hounds in full cry. They are connected with the story of Bowerman, the hunter, whose petrified figure stands about a mile north, and the Devil's Wisht Hounds. The tor is also reputedly the haunt of a phantom hound from Hell, which raced across the moor to howl around the tomb of Richard Cabell at Buckfastleigh. The story of wicked squire Cabell, who died in 1677 having sold his soul to the Devil, is thought to have provided the inspiration and the setting for Sir Arthur Conan Doyle's *The Hound of the Baskervilles* (1902). A short distance south-east of Hound Tor are the remains of a deserted medieval village dating from 1200 to 1350. Excavation in the 1960s revealed evidence that beneath the stone buildings lay a series of turf-walled dwellings dating back to the tenth or eleventh century. The outlying medieval farmstead to the north was built within a prehistoric enclosure. The distant peak in the photograph is Haytor.

GRIMSPOUND
from Hookney Tor

Lying in a saddle between Hameldown Tor and Hookney Tor, in the parish of Manaton, are the remains of the Bronze Age settlement of Grimspound, dating from 1500 to 1000 BC. At over 1500 feet above sea level, it consists of twenty-four small hut circles surrounded by a massive enclosure or 'pound'. The existence of a small stream, Grim's Lake, within the enclosure leads experts to believe that the inhabitants were pastoralists. The partly reconstructed granite walls of the pound, about three feet high and nine feet wide, enclose an area of about four acres. William Crossing wrote in his *Guide to Dartmoor*: 'When in a complete state such a barrier would ensure the safety of cattle against the attacks of wolves or other wild animals, and prove a protection for the dwellings in the pound, some of them, however, being in a very dilapidated condition, and two or three small enclosures, resembling courts, may be seen on the inner side of the wall.' Although the wall is substantial, it is not thought to have been built for defensive purposes. The huts were originally roofed with turf or thatch supported by wooden poles.

BENNET'S CROSS
Headland Warren

Beside the Moretonhamstead-to-Postbridge road, less than a mile north of Warren House Inn, Bennet's Cross is one of many upright marker stones scattered throughout Dartmoor. Roughly shaped in the form of a cross about six feet high and dating from medieval times, the granite stone bears the damaged initials W.B. for 'Warren Bounds'. It stands on an ancient packhorse track across the moor and was used as a guide stone as well as a boundary stone, marking a parish boundary and one of the 'tin bounds' for the mines of Vitifer (later Birch Tor) and Headland Warren. Why it was called Bennet's Cross is unknown. In his *Guide to Dartmoor* William Crossing notes 'that the name of William Benet occurs in the list of jurors who attended a Tinners' Parliament held on Crockern Tor in the 24th of Henry VIII, as a representative of the Stannary of Chagford'. The hill in the photograph is Birch Tor (1550 feet). On its slopes are two of a group of four stone-built enclosures, said to represent the four aces in a pack of cards dropped by the legendary Jan Reynolds after he had been claimed by the Devil.

THE GREY WETHERS
Fernworthy

On the bleak slopes of Sittaford Tor, to the west of Fernworthy Forest and some three miles north of Postbridge, are two Bronze Age stone circles known as the Grey Wethers – so called because from a distance they are said to resemble grazing grey wethers (castrated rams). Indeed there is a story, told by William Crossing in his *Guide to Dartmoor*, that one gullible farmer was tricked into buying them, believing them to be sheep: 'The bargain was struck in the Warren House Inn, and the farmer was directed to go to the newtake [enclosure] near Siddaford Tor, where he would be able to see his purchase. This he did, but unlike Bo Peep found not only that the sheep would not come home, but also that they had got no tails to bring behind them.' The circles are around 100 feet in diameter, the southernmost being the slightly larger of the two. There are about a dozen stone circles on Dartmoor, some, like Grey Wethers, thought to have been temples. Although excavation has shown that fires were lit within the circles, no trace of burials have been found.

CLAPPER BRIDGE
Postbridge

In the heart of Dartmoor, on the
Moretonhamstead-to-Princetown
road, lies the scattered hamlet of
Postbridge. It is noted for its
clapper bridge, which spans the
East Dart River just below the
present road bridge and is the
largest and most impressive in the
National Park. The bridge consists
of three massive slabs of granite
about fifteen feet long and six feet
wide, supported by four dry-laid
stone piers. Each slab may weigh
as much as eight tons. The bridge
is thought to date from the
thirteenth century. The absence of
sides allowed plenty of space for
heavily laden animals. William
Crossing notes that he had 'heard
inhabitants of Dartmoor refer to
the old tracks as post-roads, and
the clapper in question being on
the most important of these, the
forerunner of the present highway
from Plymouth and Tavistock to
Chagford and Moreton, would no
doubt be spoken of as the
post-bridge'. Two miles north-east
of Postbridge is Warren House
Inn, named after the nearby
rabbit-breeding site of Headland
Warren. Said to be the third
highest inn in England, it stands
on the opposite side of the road to
the original inn, which burnt down
in 1845.

WISTMAN'S WOOD
Two Bridges

Wistman's Wood (1300 feet above
sea level) is shrouded in mystery
and legend. The trees, primarily
pedunculate oak, *Quercus robur*,
are strangely gnarled and stunted,
averaging about fifteen feet in
height, and the most ancient are
about five hundred years old. They
grow on a west-facing slope of
clitter overlooking the West Dart
River, almost two miles north of
Two Bridges. The twisted
branches and granite boulders are
cloaked with a rich velvet covering
of mosses, lichens, liverworts and
ferns. Reputed to be one of the
most haunted places in Dartmoor,
the wood is associated with the
Devil's Wisht Hounds, spectral
black dogs with red eyes. Anyone
seeing them is said to be doomed
to die within a year. The wood,
owned by the Duchy of Cornwall,
is now a nature reserve. Similar
ancient woods can be found at
Piles Copse, two miles north of
Harford, and Black Tor Copse,
two miles south of Meldon. The
Tinners' Parliament met on nearby
Crockern Tor, to which
representatives were sent from the
stannary towns of Tavistock,
Plympton, Ashburton and
Chagford.

STONE ROWS
Merrivale

The greatest concentration of
Bronze Age monuments in Europe
can be found on the bleak,
windswept plateau of the Dartmoor
National Park. Widely distributed
throughout the moor are the
remains of countless prehistoric
villages, huts, walled enclosures,
menhirs, burial chambers
(kistvaens), stone circles and stone
rows. Although the purpose of the
menhirs, circles and rows remains
a mystery, it is thought that they
had some religious or ceremonial
function. Perhaps the most
enigmatic are the stone rows, of
which there are around seventy;
most are either single or double
rows but there are a few triples.
The longest of these granite
'avenues' or 'alignments' runs
north for over two miles from Stall
Moor across the River Erme to
Green Hill. There are three on
Long Ash Hill near the village of
Merrivale, at the western edge of
the moor, two of which run
roughly parallel to each other in an
east-west direction (one for 596 feet
and the other for 865 feet). Nearby
are a stone circle, a menhir and
several burial cairns.

MENHIR
Merrivale

Among the numerous Bronze Age
remains near Merrivale are several
menhirs or standing stones. This
one is about ten feet high and on
the horizon is a stone circle. Some
standing stones were used as
waymarkers or guide stones to
prevent travellers becoming lost
while crossing the moors. In 1696
an Act of Parliament permitted the
erection of stones or posts
engraved with a single letter
indicating the name of the next
town. The ancient track from
Ashburton to Tavistock was,
therefore, marked by a series of
guide stones bearing an 'A' on one
side and a 'T' on the other. A
number of waymarkers can be
discovered among the stones at
Merrivale; some have been
removed and re-erected as
gateposts. It is traditionally held
that when Tavistock was struck by
the plague in 1625 some of the
Merrivale stone circles were used
as a marketplace. In order to avoid
contamination, people from
surrounding villages left goods in
the circles for the citizens of
Tavistock to collect. As a further
precaution against infection,
money for payment was left in
bowls of water. Over 200 years
later the circles were still known as
'The Potato Market'.

WHEAL BETSY
Mary Tavy

On Black Down, at the western edge of Dartmoor between Lydford and Mary Tavy, is an abandoned silver, lead and copper mine known as Wheal Betsy. 'Wheal' is an old West Country word meaning a mine. Shaft mining was introduced in the fifteenth century and not only men but women and children worked deep underground to extract the various ores. Reopened in 1806, the Wheal Betsy mine (known also as Prince Arthur Mine or North Wheal Friendship) was worked by water power until the erection of an engine house and chimney stack in 1868. Before its closure in 1877, all pumping, winding and crushing of the ore was carried out by a steam-powered Cornish beam pumping engine. In 1967 the National Trust acquired the ruined engine house, made it safe and dedicated it to the memory of the mining industry of Dartmoor. The Wheal Friendship Mine at nearby Mary Tavy produced lead, iron and copper during the eighteenth and nineteenth centuries. Despite its closure in the 1870s, arsenic continued to be produced there until 1925.

WHITE LADY WATERFALL
Lydford Gorge

Rising on Bridestowe and Sourton Common, in the north-western corner of Dartmoor, the waters of the River Lyd flow south-west past the ancient fortified town of Lydford and on through Lydford Gorge. Owned by the National Trust, the oak-wooded ravine is a haven for a great variety of wildlife. There are two entrances to the gorge. Near the main entrance the Lyd tumbles through a narrow, rocky chasm to bubble and boil in a large pothole known as the Devil's Cauldron. By the other entrance is the ninety-foot-high White Lady waterfall, formed by a tributary stream. Legend says that those who fall into the river and see the ghost of a woman dressed in white will be saved from drowning. From the fifteenth to the seventeenth century the gorge was the home of the Gubbins, a wild tribe of savages who, according to Thomas Fuller (1608–61), lived 'in cotts (rather holes than houses) like swine, having all in common, multiplied without marriage into many hundreds . . . Their wealth consists in other men's goods, and they live by stealing sheep on the moor'. The Lyd joins the Tamar near Launceston and eventually enters the English Channel at Plymouth.

ST MICHAEL DE RUPE
Brentor

On the summit of Brentor – the most westerly 'tor' on Dartmoor – are the earthwork remains of an Iron Age hillfort and the medieval church of St Michael de Rupe or St Michael of the Rock. Standing 1130 feet above sea level on an eroded cone of volcanic lava (not granite), the church was once used as a distant landmark by sailors heading for Plymouth Sound. First built by Robert Giffard *c.* 1130 and rebuilt in the late thirteenth or early fourteenth century, the church is one of the smallest in England, thirty-seven feet long and fourteen-and-a-half feet wide. The thirty-two-foot-high west tower was added or rebuilt in the fifteenth century. After visiting the church, Richard Polwhele wrote in his *History of Devonshire* (1806): 'It has been shrewdly said of the inhabitants of this parish, that they make weekly atonement for their sins: for they can never go to church without the previous penance of climbing up this steep, which they are so often obliged to attempt with the weariest industry, and in the lowest attitude. In windy or rainy weather, the worthy pastor himself is frequently obliged to humble himself upon all fours, preparatory to his being exalted in the pulpit.'

OKEHAMPTON CASTLE

The ancient market town of Okehampton nestles in a valley near the confluence of the East and West Okement rivers, just outside the northern boundary of the Dartmoor National Park. The crumbling ruins of the castle, however, are just within the Park. First mentioned in the *Domesday Book*, the castle belonged to Baldwin de Brionne, Sheriff of Devon from 1069 to 1071, who died *c.* 1090. It stands on a spur of shale overlooking the valley of the West Okement, strategically sited to control a nearby river crossing. In the early fourteenth century the fortress was almost totally rebuilt by Hugh Courtenay II (created Earl of Devon in 1335), whose family held the estate, with some interruption, from the late twelfth century until 1538. The following year Henry VIII executed Hugh's descendant Henry, Marquis of Exeter, for conspiracy and confiscated the Courtenay estates. The castle, mainly built of local granite and shale, was probably dismantled shortly afterwards. It has been in the care of English Heritage since 1984. The ruins are said to be haunted by the ghost of 'Lady Howard of Fitzford'.

SCORHILL CIRCLE
near Gidleigh

One of the largest and least disturbed of the dozen or so Bronze Age stone circles on Dartmoor, Scorhill Circle is situated on the western slopes of Scorhill Tor, above the confluence of the Walla Brook and North Teign River. Consisting of twenty-four standing stones (the tallest being eight feet high) and eight fallen ones, the circle is ninety feet in diameter. The Walla Brook is spanned by a single slab of granite fifteen feet long, almost three feet wide and over a foot-and-a-half thick. Near a similar clapper bridge, spanning the North Teign, is the Tolmen Stone, a large block of granite through which the action of water has created a number of holes, the largest being about three feet in diameter. A three-mile walk to the west of Scorhill, across tracts of peat bog and past Watern Tor and Hangingstone Hill, leads to Cranmere Pool, famous for its remote moorland letterbox. Since 1854, when James Perrott of Chagford left a bottle here (later replaced by a box) for visitors to put their cards inside, hundreds of boxes containing a rubber stamp, inkpad and visitor's book have been hidden all over the moor for enthusiasts to find.

CASTLE DROGO
Drewsteignton

Built between 1910 and 1930, Castle Drogo was designed by the architect Edwin Lutyens for Julius Drewe, who made his fortune as a partner in the 'Home and Colonial Stores'. Standing on a rocky spur above the wooded valley of the River Teign, about a mile south-west of Drewsteignton, the granite building seen today is only about a third of the size of the grandiose fortress that Lutyens and Drewe had originally conceived. Having retired a millionaire in 1889 at the age of thirty-three, Drewe went to live in Sussex. Researching his ancestry, he was led to believe that he was a descendant of the Norman baron Drogo de Teign, who gave his name to the village of Drewsteignton, and eventually he bought the Drogo estate. He died in 1931, shortly after his dream of becoming a landed country gentleman had been fulfilled. The Drewe family continue to live in the castle, despite granting the property to the National Trust in 1974. Above the tower entrance, with its working portcullis, is the motto 'DROGO NOMEN ET VIRTUS ARMA DEDIT' (Drewe is the Name and Valour gave it Arms). The castle and grounds are open to the public.

Exeter and South-Eastern Devon

Sited on a small hill near a ford across the River Exe or 'Eisca', the settlement of the Celtic tribe of the Dumnonii developed into the fortified Roman city of Isca Dumnoniorum. Excavations near the cathedral in 1971–4 revealed evidence of a Roman bath house *c.* AD 60 and a basilica of later date. A Saxon monastery was built in 670 on the site of the Roman forum. The church, built by King Athelstan in 932, was destroyed by the Danes in 1003 and rebuilt by King Canute in 1019. It became a cathedral in 1050 when Bishop Leofric transferred his see from Crediton to Exeter. After the Conquest the Normans built Rougemont castle on a hill at the north-east corner of the walled city; all that now remains is the sandstone gatehouse. William I's nephew, Bishop William Warelwast, started to build the Norman cathedral with its twin towers in 1112. A new cathedral in the Decorated style, incorporating parts of the old, was begun *c.* 1275 by Bishop Walter Branscombe – whose tomb is in the Lady Chapel – and was finished in the 1340s. The west front has a long screen of statues depicting kings, saints and angels.

I n *Devon* (Pevsner's Buildings of England series) Alec Clifton Taylor wrote: 'No English county contains so great a variety of building materials as Devon. No English cathedral incorporates so many different kinds of stone as Exeter.'

The great variety of building material found throughout the West Country tends to reflect the complex geological structure of the region. Because the traditional materials – stone and cob – were usually dug locally, most of the rural farms, houses and cottages were constructed out of the rocks and soils occurring in their particular area.

Granite structures are, therefore, found around Dartmoor, Bodmin Moor, the Land's End peninsula, Hensbarrow Downs and Carnmenellis. Because the stone is coarse-grained it is unsuitable for fine carving or decorative embellishment. The colour ranges from light silver grey to pink. Being intensely hard, granite was not quarried on a large scale until the industrial advances of the late eighteenth and nineteenth centuries. Previously builders used 'moorstone', the name given to the granite slabs and boulders found around the moors and hills. Moorstone was used to construct the distinctive Dartmoor farmhouse, or longhouse, a dual-purpose building combining a house with an animal shelter or 'shippon'. It was also used for walls, gateposts and bridges.

Sandstone, of which there are at least five varieties in the region, occurs in North Cornwall and large areas of Exmoor. In Devon, where the sedimentary rock is widely distributed, the youngest sandstones are found in the eastern part of the county, while the older Devonian sandstones outcrop towards the northern and southern coasts. Limestone, another sedimentary rock, appears in Devon in two kinds: Beer freestone, a Cretaceous limestone found on the south-east coast and quarried near the Devon fishing village from which it takes its name; and the older and tougher Devonian limestones used predominantly in the buildings of Newton Abbot, Plymouth and Torquay.

Among other less familiar types of stone used as a building material in the region are the granite-like elvan, a quartz-porphyry, found on Roborough Down, near Buckland Abbey and near Mevagissey; basalt, a volcanic lava quarried at Northernhay and used by the Romans for Exeter's town walls and by the Normans for Rougemont Castle; catacleuse, a variety of greenstone which can be carved and polished, found at Cataclews Point, near Padstow; serpentine, the principal rock of the Lizard peninsula, which, because it is prone to flaws, is unreliable as a building stone but is ideal for polishing; dolerite, a green volcanic rock, found at Cornworthy near Totnes and used in parts of Dartmouth Castle; chert, a flint-like rock, found near Launceston and east of Exeter; and Hurdwick stone, a grey-green volcanic rock, of which central Tavistock is largely built.

Slate, mainly used for roofing tiles, occurs in various locations throughout the region. Devon slate, however, is not as tough and durable as the slate found at Delabole, near Camelford, North Cornwall, where it has been quarried since Elizabethan times. Much of the older Devon slate has, therefore, had to be replaced with tougher Cornish or Welsh slate. As a further protection against the weather, the walls of some houses were also hung with slate. The other main roofing material was thatch, usually wheat straw, but heather was sometimes used around the moorland areas. Thatch has also been used to cap hayricks, garden walls, barns, pig houses and roadside shelters. Because it only needs a lightweight structure to support it, thatch is ideally suited for roofing a building of cob, whose unbaked earth walls are not very strong and, unless buttressed, tend to bulge out or even collapse under a heavier weight.

Although not restricted to the West Country, cob is known to have been commonly used for rural buildings in the region from the thirteenth century until well into the nineteenth. The variations of cob – the additives needed to make the earth set, the techniques employed to build with the material and the thickness of the walls – were determined by the basic composition of the soil. In Devon, where the greatest number of cob houses and cottages still survive, the soil is mostly composed of clay, shale and sandstones from the Carboniferous period, known as the Culm Measures. Cob consists of a carefully blended mixture of soils (containing enough lime to enable it to set) together with water, chopped straw and, occasionally, small pebbles, sand and animal dung. Resting on stone or slate foundations, the cob walls were built up in layers, each of which had to be allowed to dry out thoroughly before adding the next. The foundations and the base of the walls were about three or four feet thick. The work was done entirely by eye and could take up to a year or more to complete. Houses built of cob, despite being white- or colour-washed, can be easily recognized by their rounded corners and undulating walls.

BASCLOSE
Otterton

A small tributary of the River Otter (from which Otterton takes its name) runs in a culvert along the main street of the village, past a number of traditional whitewashed cob-and-thatch cottages. 'Basclose', once the home of the coal merchant, bears the date 1627 on its stone chimney stack. Thomas Cox wrote in 1720: 'Otterton, called in ancient writings *Articumba*, which manor from the Conquest, to the Dissolution of the Abbeys, was always in the hands of religious men.' Otterton priory, a cell of the Bendictine monastery of Mont St Michel in Normandy, became the property of the Bridgettine monastery of Twickenham, founded in 1415 and later moved to Syon Abbey, near Isleworth. Traces of the priory buildings can be found near the parish church of St Michael (rebuilt in 1871 but retaining its medieval red sandstone tower). Leland wrote: 'Otterton a pretty fisher town standeth on the east side of the haven about a mile from Ottermouth.' It ceased to be a port when the river silted up in the fifteenth century. Otterton Mill, restored to working order in 1977, is open to the public, together with a bakery, shop, restaurant, museum, exhibition gallery and studio workshops.

TEIGNMOUTH
from Shaldon

The seaport of Teignmouth, lying opposite Shaldon at the mouth of the River Teign, developed as a holiday resort in the late eighteenth century. Leland, writing *c.*1540, said: 'The east point of this haven is called the Poles. This is a low sandy ground either cast out by the spring of sand out of Teign, or else thrown up from the shores by rage of wind and water: and this sand occupieth now a great quantity of ground between Teignmouth town, where the ground mounteth, and Teignmouth haven.' The original settlement was attacked by the Danes in the ninth and tenth centuries. It is said that the nearby cliffs owe their redness to the blood spilt in the slaughter of 970. Further attacks came from the French in 1347 and 1690. The church of St James dates from the late thirteenth century but was greatly restored during the nineteenth. The octagonal body of the church was built in 1817–21. John Keats stayed in the town in 1818 and moaned about the Devon weather, calling it 'a splashy, rainy, misty, snowy, foggy, haily, floody, muddy, slipshod county'. Although Dartmoor granite is no longer shipped from the port, the export of Teign valley ball clay continues.

DAWLISH
from Langstone Rock

The old village of Dawlish, centred around the parish church, lay about a mile inland, near a ford across the Dawlish Water, or 'black stream'. It began to attract visitors towards the end of the eighteenth century and, in consequence, houses were built in the valley, nearer the sea. Between 1803 and 1810 the stream was straightened and made to flow over a series of small artificial waterfalls. The little park through which it runs is known as the Lawn and forms the centrepiece of the present town. Obscuring the view of the sea is the Exeter to Plymouth railway, opened between 1846 and 1848. The stretch between Exeter and Newton Abbot was originally part of a system built to power trains by Brunel's invention of the 'atmospheric railway'. This involved a continuous pipe laid between the rails, into which fitted a piston attached to the leading vehicle in the train. Pumping houses at regular intervals along the line sucked air out of the pipe, creating a vacuum. Incoming air, entering the pipe naturally behind the piston, pushed the train along. Beset with problems, the system was soon abandoned. There is an exhibition with working models at Starcross, three miles away.

A La Ronde
Exmouth

Built in 1798 by two spinster cousins, Jane and Mary Parminter, after their return from a ten-year Grand Tour of Europe, the sixteen-sided house 'A La Ronde' was designed with rooms arranged round a central octagonal hall. The inspiration for this unique *cottage orné*, originally thatched but now tiled, came from the sixth-century church of San Vitale in Ravenna, Italy. The interior walls of the gallery at the top of the house and the staircase leading to it are decorated with feathers and shells of every shape, colour and size, presumably inspired by San Vitale's Byzantine mosaics. Other rooms, particularly the drawing room, contain artwork made from sand, seaweed, shells and paper. A La Ronde was acquired by the National Trust in 1991, and an appeal to help finance essential repair and conservation work was launched. At the time it was described as 'an example of Regency taste that is at once bizarre and intriguing, amateur and intellectual, rustic and cosmopolitan'. The tiny chapel, almshouses and former school called 'Point in View' a little higher up Summer Lane were built by the Parminters in 1811. Both cousins are buried in the chapel.

High Peak and Exmouth
from Peak Hill

Rising on Exmoor, only five miles inland from the Bristol Channel, the River Exe meanders in a southerly direction to Tiverton, Exeter and the south Devon coast. Below Topsham the sixty-mile-long river forms a wide estuary at the mouth of which – on opposite banks – are Dawlish Warren and Exmouth, both celebrated for their golden sands. Leland noted *c.* 1540 that Exmouth was 'a fisher townlet a little within the haven mouth'. Later that century the ancient port was used as a base by Sir Walter Raleigh. The town's development as a holiday resort began in the 1790s with the building of a row of Georgian houses known as the Beacon. According to Pevsner, the town's two most interesting houses are A La Ronde and the Barn (now a hotel). The latter, in Foxholes Road, was designed in 1896 by Edward Schroeder Prior – an exponent of the Arts and Crafts Movement – in a butterfly plan. It was burnt down in 1905 and rebuilt. The roof, now slate, was originally thatched. The promenade, two miles long, leads east from the harbour and docks towards the red sandstone cliffs of the High Land of Orcombe. Further east, at Sandy Bay, is a museum of Country Life.

SIDMOUTH
from Peak Hill

Spreading inland up the valley of
the little River Sid and sheltered
by Peak Hill and Salcombe Hill,
Sidmouth was originally a small
fishing town. Thomas Cox wrote in
1720 that it was 'a port of some
considerable account, but it is now
choked up so much by sands cast
into it by the tides, that no ships of
burden can get in; yet it remains
one of the chief fisher towns in the
shire, and furnisheth those eastern
parts with much provision'. It
became a fashionable resort during
the late eighteenth and early
nineteenth centuries due to the
patronage of wealthy merchants
and members of the nobility. The
Duke and Duchess of Kent, with
their infant daughter, the future
Queen Victoria, stayed at what is
now the Royal Glen Hotel from
Christmas Eve 1819 until the
duke's death in January 1920.
Much of the town's architecture
dates from the Georgian and
Regency periods. Sidmouth, which
has almost 500 listed buildings, is
also noted for its 'picturesque'
dwellings or *cottages ornés*. Usually
thatched, these cottages were often
elaborately decorated with Gothic
windows, fretworked bargeboards,
deep projecting eaves and tall
chimneys. An international folk
festival is held here annually.

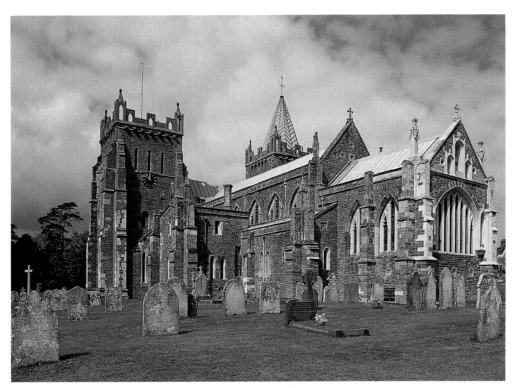

PARISH CHURCH
Ottery St Mary

On the eastern side of the River
Otter (from which it takes its
name) lies the market town of
Ottery St Mary, which dates back
to Saxon times. On a hilltop site,
the present church of St Mary
began as a small parish church,
but was enlarged by John de
Grandisson, Bishop of Exeter,
between 1338 and 1342 and is
modelled on Exeter Cathedral. It
flourished as a collegiate church
from the mid-fourteenth century
until its dissolution in 1545. The
school was refounded by Henry
VIII as the 'Kynge's Newe
Grammer Scole of Seynt Marie
Oterey'. The Revd John Coleridge
was appointed master of King's
School and vicar of the parish in
1760, holding both positions until
his death in 1781. The youngest of
his thirteen children by two wives
was Samuel Taylor Coleridge, who
was born in the 'public School
House' in 1772. During the
seventeenth and eighteenth
centuries the town was noted for
the manufacture of serges, and this
was superseded by a flourishing
silk industry. The serge factory in
Mill Street, built in 1788–9, had
the largest waterwheel in England,
eighteen feet in diameter;
constructed in 1790, the circular
'tumbling weir' is thought to
be unique.

HOOKEN CLIFFS
from Beer Head

One night in March 1790 a 600-yard stretch of chalk cliffs between Beer Head and Branscombe Mouth slipped about 250 feet towards the sea, creating the distinctive white columns known as the Pinnacles. Hooken Cliffs, where the landslip occurred, rise to over 400 feet. This is the most westerly chalk headland in England. Here the 594-mile South West Coast Path from Minehead to Poole offers a choice of routes: one path runs along the top of Hooken Cliffs, passing the old coastguard's lookout; the other zigzags steeply across the landslip beneath the cliffs. At Berry Cliff, further along the coast beyond Branscombe Mouth, are the earthwork remains of a prehistoric enclosure, possibly an Iron Age fort. To the west of Branscombe Mouth chalk was quarried for lime burning, some being shipped along the coast and some being burnt in nearby kilns. Beer stone has been quarried in the area since Roman times, and was used extensively in the building of Exeter Cathedral, having been shipped from the village of Beer by sea and river. The underground quarry, about a mile west of Beer, is open to the public. Some passages lead to the sea and are reputed to have been used by local smugglers.

COOMBE AND LONG VIEW COTTAGES
Branscombe

Strung out for over two miles along three branching wooded coombes that lead down to the shingle beach of Branscombe Mouth, the ancient village of Branscombe was once dependent on lace-making, fishing and smuggling. In the graveyard at St Winifred's church is a tomb to John Hurley, a local Customs House Officer who 'fell by some means or other from the top of the cliff to the bottom by which he was unfortunately killed'. The inscription states that he was 'endeavouring to extinguish some fire made between Beer and Seaton as a signal to a smuggling boat then off at sea'. The church, incorporating parts of an earlier Saxon foundation, dates from *c*. 1130 with later alterations and additions. Inside is an eighteenth-century three-decker pulpit surmounted by a golden torch and the tomb of Joan Wadham (d. 1583), whose son Nicholas founded Wadham College, Oxford. The thatched cottages in the photograph stand near the church. Among other buildings of interest are the Mason's Arms, the medieval 'Church Living', the smithy and the old village bakery, now a museum and tearoom belonging to the National Trust.

PARISH CHURCH
Cullompton

The old market and wool-manufacturing town of Cullompton lies ten miles north-east of Exeter, on the west side of the River Culm, a tributary of the Exe. The church of St Andrew, built of local red sandstone and embellished with carvings in lighter Beer and Ham Hill stone, dates from the fifteenth century. The 100-foot-high west tower was erected in 1545–9 while the lavishly decorated outer south aisle was added *c.*1526 by John Lane, a wealthy cloth merchant. Among other items of interest are the brightly painted rood screen which stretches over fifty feet across the church; the unique 'Golgotha', a great rock-like oak block (now in two pieces) roughly carved with bones and skulls, which has sockets to support the foot of the crucifix and rood figures; the carved and coloured wagon roof; the long Jacobean west gallery, supported on Ionic columns. The church, restored in 1848–50, was one of the buildings to escape a fire in 1838 when over 200 houses were destroyed. Amongst other buildings to survive were the timbered Manor House, dated 1603, and Walronds, built of sandstone with two wings and dated 1605. Both are in Fore Street.

BICKLEIGH

The village of Bickleigh – in the wooded valley of the River Exe, some four miles south of Tiverton – houses two famous Devon pubs, the Fisherman's Cott and the Trout Inn. The latter, together with the Bickleigh Cottage Country Hotel (both dating from the seventeenth century), can be seen in the photograph. A five-arched bridge, spanning the fast-flowing Exe, was partly rebuilt after being badly damaged by a flood in 1809. It is said to be haunted by a headless horseman. Bickleigh Castle, on the west bank of the river, is of Norman origin. Much of the fortified manor house was destroyed by the Parliamentarians under General Fairfax during the Civil War. The gatehouse, which survived, dates from the fourteenth century. Part of the former moat has been turned into a water garden. The thatched cob farmhouse was built after the Restoration to replace the demolished north wing. The castle is open to the public. Across the road is a thatched Norman chapel dating from *c.*1090. Among the many attractions at Bickleigh Mill Devonshire's Centre are craft workshops, an agricultural and bygones museum, a working nineteenth-century farm and a restored water-mill.

Ilfracombe and Northern Devon

ILFRACOMBE
from Hillsborough

Contained between the dominant heights of the Torrs and Hillsborough, with its Iron Age cliff castle, Ilfracombe's mainly Victorian houses and hotels climb up the steep hillsides in terraces from the harbour. In 1720 Thomas Cox noted that the town had a 'pretty safe Harbour for Ships, by reason of a Pile built there. It is remarkable for the Lights here maintained, instead of a Watch-Tower, for the Direction of Sailors.' On Lantern Hill, overlooking the harbour, the restored chapel of St Nicholas, built in the fourteenth century for seamen, has been used as a lighthouse since at least 1522. An ancient market town as well as a former shipbuilding port, Ilfracombe became a holiday resort in the early nineteenth century. Its main growth, however, was due to the arrival of the railway in 1874, which not only brought Victorian tourists but doubled the population. The Tunnels Bathing Beaches, reached by tunnels cut through the cliffs, were opened to the public in 1836 with separate pools for men and women. Only one of these pools remains. Among the many local attractions are Ilfracombe Museum, Hele Mill and Chambercombe Manor.

Despite the fact that smuggling, or 'fair trading' as it was called, was prevalent all round the English coast, it was in the West Country that the practice was most notorious. Even place names bear witness to the trade: near Ilfracombe, for example, can be found Samson's Bay, named after a local smuggler, and Brandy Cove. The main factors which contributed to the trade's growth into an organized and widespread operation in the region were twofold: the lack of prevention and the extreme poverty of the inhabitants. The early smugglers were illegal exporters rather than importers, trading mainly in tin. With the introduction of export duties on wool in the late thirteenth century came the need to recruit customs officials to collect the dues. Over the following centuries further taxes were levied on wine, tobacco, tea, spirits, silks and other goods. The imposition of a salt tax in the late seventeenth century made smuggling an economic necessity for most poverty-stricken West Country fishermen. Without salt for curing pilchards (their main source of winter food) many families would not have been able to survive.

Smuggling, which reached its height during the eighteenth century, was not, however, restricted to the poor. All levels of society were involved in the trade, including tinners, magistrates, squires and parsons – none regarding their actions as criminal – and even excise men were invariably open to bribes. Although smuggling was by no means the romantic activity it has been made to appear by novelists and film-makers, almost every coastal village or port had its local hero; probably the most famous was John Carter, nicknamed the 'King of Prussia', after whom Prussia Cove was named.

Making use of the long and indented coastline, with its narrow inlets, wooded creeks, secluded coves and cave-riddled cliffs, the smugglers would bring the contraband ashore and stow it in secret hideaways. Not only individuals but whole communities were involved. In Devon some people set the end of a bottle in the walls of their cottages, just below the eaves, to show that they were willing to assist 'fair traders'. On occasion people were forced into the trade by ruthless individuals like Thomas Benson of Bideford, MP for Barnstaple. Finding himself in charge of transporting convicts to America, Benson shipped them instead to Lundy Island (having rented it in 1748), where they were employed in his smuggling organization. When found out, he reputedly told his accusers that the convicts had indeed been transported overseas according to contract.

BULL POINT LIGHTHOUSE

The coast between Lee Bay and Morte Point is one of the most treacherous in Devon, with jagged reefs of sandstones and shales, tilted almost vertically, projecting outwards from the slatey cliffs. In the days of sail numerous ships were ripped apart on the deadly rocks. Not surprisingly, this remote coastline was associated with smuggling and wrecking. A saying reflects the fear once felt by the locals: 'Morte is the place which heaven made last and the devil will take first.' The first lighthouse on Bull Point was opened in 1879. After cliff subsidence in 1972 it became unsafe and in 1974 the present building was constructed. It is now fully automated. The village of Lee, near the mouth of the wooded 'Fuchsia Valley', contains a number of attractive cottages, including the thatched 'Old Maids' Cottage', reputed to date from 1653. The church of St Matthew was built in the 1830s. Overlooking the rocky bay are 'Smuggler's Cottage', dated 1627, the stone-built 'Old Mill' and the former manor house (now a hotel).

SWEETS COTTAGE
Croyde

Nestling in a sheltered coombe behind the sand dunes of Croyde Bay, the village of Croyde contains a number of thatched, colour-washed cottages. Like many of them, Sweets Cottage has a small roadside stream running in front of it, with a tiny bridge giving access to the garden gate. The Gem, Rock & Shell Museum in the village contains a fascinating collection of stones and shells from all over the world. Croyde Bay is popular with surfers, and the Baggy Point headland, on the northern side of the bay, is an important rock-climbing site. Here great sheets of sandstone rise almost vertically from the sea for some 200 feet. The stepped, white post on top of the National Trust-owned headland was used to simulate the mast of a ship in coastguard training exercises with rocket-propelled life-saving apparatus. Beside the coastal path, near the Baggy Point Hotel, are the bones of a whale washed up in 1915. Tight under the cliff below, but not visible from the top, is a fifty-ton ice-smoothed boulder of granulite gneiss known as the Baggy Erratic. It is thought to have been deposited on the shore platform in the Ice Age and possibly originated in Scotland.

ARLINGTON COURT

The main block of the present
Arlington Court, with its severely
plain neo-classical exterior, was
built in 1820 for Colonel John
Chichester to designs by Thomas
Lee, a Barnstaple architect. Sir
Bruce Chichester, the colonel's
grandson, enlarged the hall and
added the north wing in 1865. The
Chichester family owned Arlington
Court from the sixteenth century
until 1949, when the house and its
contents, together with some 3000
acres of surrounding land, was
given to the National Trust by
Miss Rosalie Chichester. During
her eighty-four years at Arlington
Court Miss Chichester, an
enthusiastic traveller, amassed a
fascinating collection of mementoes
including pewter, model ships and
stuffed birds, though only a
fraction of the treasures she
collected are on display in the
house. A remarkable watercolour
by William Blake was discovered
on top of a cupboard in 1949, and
the painting, signed and dated
1821, is on display in the
Ante-Room. Descendants of Miss
Chichester's Jacob sheep and
Shetland ponies still graze in the
wooded grounds. The property is
seven miles south-east of
Ilfracombe, on the main road from
Combe Martin to Barnstaple.

APPLEDORE
from Instow

Sharing the same peninsula as
Westward Ho! and Northam, the
'little white fishing village' of
Appledore (as the novelist Charles
Kingsley called it) overlooks
Instow and the estuaries of the
Taw and Torridge, both noted
salmon rivers. Ships have been
built here since the fourteenth
century and the tradition continues
today. A covered shipbuilding yard
– one of the largest in Europe at
the time – was opened in 1969.
Rising up the hillside, with its
fisherman's cottages, narrow
cobbled streets, and
nineteenth-century church,
Appledore was once the home of
the pirate and smuggler Thomas
Benson MP. The museum in Odun
Road, overlooking the estuary, has
a fascinating collection of exhibits
depicting the maritime history of
North Devon. Nearby Westward
Ho!, named after Kingsley's novel,
was founded in 1863. Northam
Burrows, a large stretch of sand
dunes and saltmarsh which lies to
the north-east, is now a Country
Park. It is protected from the sea
by Pebble Ridge, a natural, slowly
shifting two-mile-long rampart of
stones and boulders. At Bloody
Corner, on the Northam-to-
Appledore road, is a stone
commemorating King Hubba the
Dane, 'slain by King Alfred the
Great in a bloody retreat AD
DCCCLXXXXII [sic]'.

HARTLAND POINT
LIGHTHOUSE

Hartland Point, at the north-western tip of Devon, formed 'the boundary of the old "Severn Sea", the Channel here expanding its jaws as if to receive the rolling waves and clearer water of the Atlantic' (*Murray's Handbook*, 1859). On a ledge below the 325-foot-high headland is a small white lighthouse, opened in 1874, which emits one of the strongest lights on Britain's coast. It was converted to automatic operation in 1983. A broken and rusting hull nearby is all that remains of the motor-vessel *Johanna*, which grounded under the lighthouse in the early hours of 31 December 1982 carrying a cargo of grain. Captain and crew were safely rescued by helicopter and lifeboat. Eleven miles out in the Bristol Channel lies the granite island of Lundy, inhabited by a small working community. After it was bought by William Heaven in 1834 it became known as the 'Kingdom of Heaven'. Today the island is looked after by the Landmark Trust on behalf of the National Trust. The puffin, from which Lundy derives its name, still frequents the island. *MS Oldenburg*, the island's own ship, runs day trips to Lundy from Bideford and, during the summer, from Ilfracombe as well.

CLOVELLY

The privately owned fishing village of Clovelly, with its main cobbled street plunging steeply in broad steps down to the harbour, owes much of its present charm to the Hamlyns, who succeeded the Carys as lords of the manor in 1738. Christine Hamlyn, particularly, who owned the estate from 1884 to 1936, devoted much of her life to restoring the houses and preserving the unique character of the village. Known as the 'Queen of Clovelly', her initials can be found on many of the cottages. Vehicles have to be left in the car park at the top of the steep, wooded valley while loads, including the milk, are delivered by wooden sledges. Authorized vehicles have access to the harbour by means of a private road. The name 'Clovelly', mentioned in the *Domesday Book*, is thought to mean 'cleft or cut in a semicircular, wheel-shaped hill'. The three-mile-long Hobby Drive, east of the village, was built by Sir James Hamlyn Williams in 1811–29. The Gregg family, who lived in a sea cave nearby, were reputed to be cannibals, having eaten around 1,000 people before being executed. The earthwork remains of Clovelly Dykes, an Iron Age hillfort, are about a mile inland.

Taunton and Exmoor

OARE

Nestling in the moorland valley of the Oare Water, midway between Porlock and Lynmouth and less than two miles from the sea, the tiny village of Oare was made famous by R. D. Blackmore's *Lorna Doone*. Lorna and John Ridd were married in the church of St Mary; wearing a dress of 'pure white, clouded with faint lavender', she was shot at the altar by Carver Doone, just as the couple were about to kiss. A memorial to Blackmore, whose grandfather was rector of the parish from 1809 to 1842, can be found inside the church. Since the seventeenth century, the period in which the novel was set, the chancel has been extended and the west tower rebuilt. Plover's Barrows Farm, the home of the Ridds, has not been positively identified. Sir Atholl Oakeley, in *The Facts on which Blackmore based Lorna Doone*, claimed that it stood on the site of Oare House, a farmhouse built in 1883 on the north side of the river, opposite the church. Oare Manor, erected beside the church in 1690, was once the home of the Snow family, who first acquired the property in the early eighteenth century. Nicholas Snowe, mentioned in *Lorna Doone*, was a neighbour of the Ridds.

Samuel Taylor Coleridge (1772–1834), born at Ottery St Mary in Devon, was the youngest son of the vicar and schoolmaster. Educated at Christ's Hospital, London, and Jesus College, Cambridge, he moved to Nether Stowey on the edge of the Quantock Hills in Somerset with his wife and son in 1796. The following year William and Dorothy Wordsworth rented nearby Alfoxton Park, where Dorothy wrote her *Alfoxden Journal* and William collaborated with Coleridge on *The Lyrical Ballads* (1798). While living at Nether Stowey Coleridge often walked the eleven miles to Taunton to preach at the Unitarian chapel. Among those who visited him at his Lime Street cottage were Charles Lamb (1775–1834) and William Hazlitt (1778–1830). 'The Rime of the Ancient Mariner', among other poems, was composed while Coleridge was living at Nether Stowey. 'Kubla Khan' – interrupted by a person from Porlock – was written after a dream in one of the farmhouses around Culbone, Exmoor.

The moor provided the setting for R. D. Blackmore's historical novel *Lorna Doone: A Romance of Exmoor* (1869). The story was based on the legends of the Doones of 'Bagworthy', a gang of Scottish outlaws who settled on Exmoor in the seventeenth century. Born at Longworth, Oxfordshire, Blackmore (1825–1900) moved to Devon in 1831 to join his father, who had become curate of Culmstock. He was educated at Blundell's School, Tiverton, and Exeter College, Oxford. Although he spent most of his adult life in London, Blackmore insisted: 'In everything, except the accident of birth, I am Devonian; my ancestry were all Devonians; my sympathies and feelings are all Devonian.'

Charles Kingsley (1819–75) was born at Holne, on the edge of Dartmoor and lived at Clovelly, North Devon, from 1831 until 1836, when his father was appointed curate and then rector of the parish. The village is 'Aberalva' in Kingsley's *Two Years Ago* (1857) and is also described in *Westward Ho! or The Voyages and Adventures of Sir Amyas Leigh, Knight* (1855). Charles Dickens (1812–70) and Wilkie Collins (1824–89) visited Clovelly in 1861. Described by Dickens as 'Steepways' in *Message from the Sea* (1860), the village became popular with Victorian visitors because of the writings of Kingsley and Dickens. Rudyard Kipling (1865–1936), born in India, was educated at the United Services College in Westward Ho! from 1878 to 1882, and *Stalky & Co.* (1899) draws on his schooldays there.

Born at Bodmin, Cornwall, in 1863, Sir Arthur Quiller-Couch, often known just as 'Q', lived at Fowey from 1892 until his death in 1944 (becoming mayor in 1937–8). *The Astonishing History of Troy Town*, published in 1888, is based on the historic seaport. He was buried in the church of St Fimbarrus (formerly dedicated to St Nicholas). Kenneth Grahame (1859–1932), often stayed with 'Q' and then went sailing on the estuary together. The river is said to have inspired much of the setting for Grahame's *The Wind in the Willows*.

Virginia Woolf (1882–1941) spent her childhood summers at St Ives. D. H. Lawrence (1885–1930) lived at Padstow and Zennor between 1915 and 1917. Winston Graham, born in Manchester in the late 1920s and author of the Poldark novels depicting Cornish life in the late eighteenth century, lived in Cornwall for thirty years from the age of sixteen. A. L. Rowse, poet, biographer and historian, was born at St Austell in 1903. Thomas Hardy (1840–1928), who trained as an architect, went in 1870 to St Juliot, two miles up the Valency valley, Boscastle, to supervise the restoration of the church and married the rector's sister-in-law, Emma Gifford, in 1874. 'Castle Boterel' in his *A Pair of Blue Eyes* (1873) is Boscastle. Dame Daphne Du Maurier (1907–89) set many of her novels and period romances in the West Country, including *Jamaica Inn* (1936), *Rebecca* (1938) and *Frenchman's Creek* (1942). She died at her clifftop home of Kilmarth, near Par, Cornwall, on 19 April 1989.

Robert Stephen Hawker (1803–75), much of whose poetry was inspired by the landscape and legends of Cornwall, was vicar of the parish of Morwenstow from 1835 to 1875. The eccentric poet-parson was the subject of Sabine Baring-Gould's *The Vicar of Morwenstow* (1876). Born in Exeter in 1834, Baring-Gould wrote extensively on the West Country, as well as writing novels and the hymn 'Onward Christian Soldiers'. He lived at Lew Trenchard, where he was rector and squire, from 1881 until his death in 1924.

Dame Agatha Christie (1890–1976) was born in Barton, Torquay, and spent her childhood there. She married Archibald Christie in 1914 and, during the First World War, worked as a hospital dispenser, gaining a knowledge of poisons which she later used in her detective stories. In 1930, two years after her divorce, she married the archaeologist Max Mallowan. Eight years later she bought Greenway House, opposite Dittisham, as a summer home, visiting it every year. The house, on the banks of the River Dart, was formerly the childhood home of Sir Humphrey Gilbert, 'Father of British Colonization'.

Among other writers associated with Torquay are Elizabeth Barrett Browning (1806–61), Edward Bulwer-Lytton (1803–73), Eden Phillpotts (1862–1960) and Sir Richard Burton (1821–90). Kipling wrote in 1896: 'Torquay is such a place as I do desire to upset by dancing through it with nothing on but my spectacles.' Between 1928 and 1947

Flora Thompson (1876–1947) lived first at Dartmouth, then at Brixham. Sir Thomas Bodley (1545–1613), who refounded the Bodleian Library, Oxford, in 1602, was born in Exeter, and The Bodley Head publishing house, founded by John Lane and Charles Elkin Mathews in 1887, was named after him. The River Torridge, which rises on the moorland south of Hartland, provided the setting for *Tarka the Otter* (1927), written by Henry Williamson (1895–1977) who moved to Devon in 1921.

Sir John Betjeman (1906–84), born in Highgate, London, visited Cornwall many times during his childhood and, as an adult, returned to the county regularly, taking a holiday home at Trebetherick. In his autobiographical poem 'Summoned by Bells' (1960), he describes how, as a boy, he used to explore the 'dear lanes of Cornwall', riding for miles on his bicycle to 'far-off churches' with 'a one-inch map' and 'well-worn *Little Guide*'. Poet Laureate and defender of the architectural heritage of Britain, Betjeman's first guidebook, *Cornwall* (Shell Guide), was published in 1934, to be followed by *Devon* (Shell Guide) two years later. He is buried in St Enodoc's churchyard, Trebetherick, near Polzeath. The church inspired two of Betjeman's poems, 'Sunday Afternoon Service in St Enodoc Church, Cornwall' (published in *New Bats in Old Belfries*, 1945) and 'By the Ninth Green, St Enodoc' (published in *High and Low*, 1966). Betjeman said that 'the old and beautiful Cornwall is now mostly to be found on foot'. The old and beautiful West Country may also be found writ large within the poetry and prose of its much respected writers.

RUGGED JACK
Valley of the Rocks

Running parallel to the coast for over a mile, from Lynton in the east to Wringcliff Bay in the west, the Valley of the Rocks is dominated by the rocky sandstone tors of Rugged Jack, Castle Rock and the Devil's Cheese Ring. Experts suggest that the valley may have been the old bed of the East Lyn River which dried up as sea levels rose (during the last 250,000 years), giving the river a new outlet at Lynmouth. William Hazlitt who, with Coleridge, walked some forty miles here from the Quantocks in 1798, described the place as 'bedded among precipices overhanging the sea, with rocky caverns beneath, into which the waves dash, and where the seagull for ever wheels its screaming flight'. Rugged Jack is said to be named after a Lynton youth who was turned to stone by the Devil for missing church one Sunday. The hole on the summit of Castle Rock, when seen against the sky, reveals the silhouette of the legendary White Lady who haunted the wicked Black Abbot of Lynton at the time of the Crusades. Mother Meldrum in *Lorna Doone* is reputedly based on Aggie Norman, who lived in a hovel on the rock. The wild Cheviot goats were introduced in the early 1980s.

MARS HILL
Lynmouth

On the night of Friday 15 August 1952 heavy, incessant rain, coupled with a massive cloudburst over the hills of Exmoor, almost completely destroyed the village of Lynmouth on the coast. Raging flood water, carrying tons of debris before it, hurtled down the valleys of the East and West Lyn Rivers to converge on the small fishing village, ripping out for itself 'a new course – the high street of Lynmouth', as *The Times* of 18 August described. 'There, along this tragic street of desolation, are the boulders, and the trees, like spent ammunition that ancient gods might have hurled down from aloft.' The toll of that tragic night was terrible: thirty-four people killed, ninety-three houses and buildings destroyed and twenty-eight bridges swept away. Today, after the clearance of 114,000 tons of debris and much rebuilding, including straightening and deepening the river bed, the scars have healed. Lynmouth was described by Southey as resembling a 'Swiss village', and one of its oldest parts is Mars Hill, at the foot of which is the Rising Sun Hotel, where Blackmore stayed while researching *Lorna Doone*. The cliff railway, with a gradient of 1 in 1.75, opened in 1890 and links Lynmouth with Lynton, 500 feet above.

WATERFALLS
Watersmeet

Fed by numerous moorland streams, the Hoar Oak Water and the East Lyn River join at Watersmeet, some two miles south-east of Lynmouth. The estate, owned by the National Trust, contains mainly sessile oak woodland, tumbling, dipper-frequented waters and steep, rocky cliffs. Watersmeet House, now accommodating a restaurant and shop, was built by the Halliday family *c.* 1830 as a fishing and shooting lodge, using locally quarried stone. The nearby lime kilns were operational in the early nineteenth century, burning limestone with coal to produce quicklime for agricultural use. The raw material, having been shipped to Lynmouth from South Wales, was carried inland by packhorse and mule to the kilns. Many of the paths on the estate originated as mule or donkey tracks during the heyday of the charcoal and tanning industries. The coppiced oak trees were cut down every twenty-five years or so and the wood used for fences, hurdles and even pit props in the Welsh coal mines. The bark was used in tanning. All the bridges in the area were swept away during the 1952 flood disaster, when enormous landslips deposited hundreds of trees and boulders into the rivers.

OARE COMMON
from Yenworthy Common

The landscape of Exmoor, the smallest National Park in England, largely comprises wild expanses of heather, bracken and grassy moorland, high arable farmland and deep wooded coombes. Like Dartmoor, it is noted for its semi-wild ponies, the Exmoor breed dating from prehistoric times. With their thick, wiry coats, insulated by a dense undercoat, these small hardy animals (which all have owners) are able to survive on the moors even in the coldest winters. Herds of the pure-bred Exmoor pony can be found on Withypool Common, Winsford Hill and Haddon Hill, above Wimbleball Lake, amongst other places. Each October the animals are rounded up and branded. The wooded valleys and open moorland are also inhabited by Britain's largest wild animal, the red deer, which has been adopted as the emblem of the National Park. This elusive creature sheds its antlers once a year in the spring, and in the autumn the woods and valleys echo to the eerie bellowing and clashing antlers of rutting stags. Exmoor supports the largest herd of red deer in England and Wales. Birds on Exmoor include the raven, blackcock, buzzard, nightjar, peregrine falcon and merlin.

PARISH CHURCH
Culbone

Hidden in a deep and remote wooded coombe 400 feet above sea level, some two miles west of Porlock Weir, the tiny parish church of Culbone is thought to have been built in the late twelfth century, incorporating parts of an earlier Saxon structure. Later alterations and additions include the thirteenth-century porch and the late fourteenth-century rood screen. The little slate spire, added in the early nineteenth century, is said by 'waggish people' to have been 'snipped off from the top of Porlock church' (church guide). *The Guinness Book of Records* enters it as the 'smallest completed medieval English church in regular use', measuring thirty-five feet by twelve feet. According to the church guide, it will seat thirty-three in 'great discomfort'. Standing on a medieval base, the present churchyard cross was erected in 1966. The name 'Culbone' is thought to be derived from 'Kil Beun', meaning the 'church of St Beuno'. It was while staying in a remote farmhouse near Culbone, possibly Withycombe Farm (now gone) or Ash Farm, that Coleridge started to write his opium-induced poem 'Kubla Khan', only to be interrupted by the anonymous person from Porlock.

TARR STEPS
River Barle

Rising on the wet, rough peat moorland of the Chains, near Pinkworthy Pond, the River Barle threads a south-easterly course – through Simonsbath, Withypool and Dulverton – to join the River Exe near Exebridge. Three miles downstream from Withypool the river is crossed by Tarr Steps, an ancient clapper bridge some 180 feet long, built with seventeen stone slabs, the largest measuring eight-and-a-half feet by five feet. The bridge is said by some to be prehistoric, by others medieval. After being almost entirely destroyed by the floods of 1952, it was painstakingly rebuilt. Legend says that the bridge was built by the Devil, who liked to sunbathe on the stones, and any person or creature disturbing him did so at their peril. One day a parson was persuaded to cross and, meeting the Devil in the centre of the bridge, he challenged the Prince of Darkness to a battle of words. Although the Devil's language was so bad that it wilted the trees in the surrounding woods, the parson responded with even worse abuse. The Devil was forced to concede defeat, leaving the bridge for travellers to pass over freely. The steps are on the route of the 103-mile-long Two Moors Way.

LANDACRE BRIDGE
near Withypool

Spanning the River Barle, two miles west of the Domesday village of Withypool, the five-arched Landacre (pronounced Lannaker) Bridge was first recorded in 1610. The old Swainmote Courts, dealing with the laws and regulations of the Royal Forest, were held here and at Hawkridge twice a year until the seventeenth century, when the meetings were moved to Simonsbath. Jeremy Stickles, the King's Messenger in *Lorna Doone*, was riding towards Landacre Bridge, accompanied by an Exeter trooper, when they were attacked by the outlaw Doones. After the trooper had fallen 'headlong into the torrent', Stickles, chased by 'three great Doones' was forced to ride 'a race for his precious life, at the peril of his limbs and neck'. The bridge at Landacre, despite taking a heavy battering, survived the devastating floods of 15 August 1952. Leland described the landscape in this remote region as 'forest, barren, and moorish ground, where is store and breeding of young cattle, but little or no corn or habitation'. Among the prehistoric remains to be found hereabouts are the Brightworthy Barrows on Withypool Common and the Bronze Age stone circle on Withypool Hill.

PARISH CHURCH
Stoke Pero

'Oare, Culbone and Stoke Pero / Are three such places you seldom hear o' ' says one old rhyme. Or, in similar vein: 'Culbone, Oare, Stoke Pero / Parishes three, where no parson'll go.' The church of Stoke Pero, at 1013 feet above sea level, is one of the highest churches on Exmoor and also one of the most remote. Possibly standing on the site of a Celtic foundation, the present church dates from the thirteenth century but was restored in 1897–8 by Sir Thomas Dyke Acland. The timber for the roof was carted from Porlock by a donkey named 'Zulu', whose picture now hangs in the church. At some unknown period the medieval tower was either lowered or left unfinished as the stairs end abruptly at the roof. The manors of Wilmersham (shown in the photograph), on the other side of the valley, and Stoke are recorded in the Domesday Book. Stoke was later named Stoke Pero after the Pirou family from Normandy, the earliest record of their presence in the parish occurring in the reign of Edward I (1272–1307). In the early nineteenth century there were 'fourteen mean-looking dwellings' near the church. Today there is only Church Farm.

VALE OF PORLOCK
from Luccombe Hill

Stretching north-west from Wootton Courtenay to Porlock Bay, the low-lying Vale of Porlock is noted for its rich pastures and arable farmland (the fields between Porlock and the three-mile stretch of grey-pebble beach being reclaimed marshland). At very low tides evidence of a submerged forest can be found. Bossington, one of the Holnicote Estate villages, contains a number of cottages built in the local vernacular style with tall chimneys and external bread ovens. Most date from the seventeenth century. The Lynch Chapel, nearby, dates from *c.* 1530. After falling into disuse it was restored in 1885 by Sir Thomas Dyke Acland. At the head of the Vale, at Tivington near Wootton Courtenay, St Leonard's Chapel-of-Ease dates from the fourteenth century. After the Dissolution it was not only used as a storehouse, a barn and a nineteenth-century 'dame-school' but a small cottage was built against the east wall. The chapel, thatched with traditional West Country wheaten reed, was restored to church use in 1896 and, unusually, contains an open fireplace. Horner Wood, to the west of the Luccombe Plantation, is a Site of Special Scientific Interest.

BOW AND PERIWINKLE COTTAGES
Selworthy

On the richly wooded slopes of Selworthy Beacon, above the fertile farmland of the Vale of Porlock, the village of Selworthy is noted for its attractive colour-washed cottages and Perpendicular church. The thatched cottages around the green were built in 1828 by Sir Thomas Dyke Acland, tenth Baronet, for retired workers and pensioners on the Holnicote Estate. Now owned by the National Trust, one of the cottages serves as a shop and information centre during the summer season while another, Periwinkle Cottage, offers teas and refreshments. Ivy's Cottage, opposite Bow Cottage, was once the home of Ivy Gwendoline Cann (1906–91), verger of the parish church for well over fifty years. The white church of All Saints, set high amidst the trees, is a prominent landmark from the Vale. Pevsner called it 'remarkably lavish for its present hidden-away position'. Its south aisle, dated 1538, he considered to be 'unsurpassed in the county'. There are various walks from the village to Selworthy Beacon (1012 feet above sea level). One route passes Bury Castle, an Iron Age hillfort, and also the stone Memorial Hut built to commemorate the tenth Baronet.

PACKHORSE BRIDGE
Allerford

The ancient settlement of Allerford, mentioned in the Domesday Book, is part of the Holnicote Estate now owned by the National Trust. Nestling beneath the wooded slopes of Selworthy Beacon almost two miles east of Porlock, the village is noted for its medieval two-arched packhorse bridge. The adjacent red sandstone cottage known as 'Meadowside', was originally thatched and has a number of typical architectural features, including a porch with a room above, a tall cylindrical chimney on the front wall and an external extension at the base of the chimney to accommodate a bread oven. The thatched nineteenth-century primary school, in use until 1981, now houses the West Somerset Rural Life Museum. Most of the trees above Allerford and Selworthy were planted in batches between 1809 and 1826 by Sir Thomas Dyke Acland, tenth Baronet, to commemorate the births of his nine children. From the ford the River Aller flows north-west to Bossington (another Holnicote Estate village) before filtering through a shingle beach into Porlock Bay.

LUCCOMBE

Once part of the Holnicote Estate, most of the village of Luccombe is now in the care of the National Trust. Nestling in a hollow below Luccombe Plantation, in the shadow of Dunkery Beacon, the village was subjected to a survey by the government-funded Mass Observation Unit in 1944–5. Much of the information collected, which included interviews with the inhabitants, was published in 1947 in *Exmoor Village* by W. J. Turner. Luccombe, thought to mean 'an enclosure in a valley', contains about forty houses, including a thatched post office and stores, and a village hall (formerly the school) but no public house. The church of St Mary the Virgin, crowned by an eighty-two-foot-high battlemented tower, dates from the thirteenth century. The memorial on the north wall, inscribed with a Latin epitaph and surmounted by a coat of arms, commemorates the Royalist Dr Henry Byam, a former vicar of both Luccombe and Selworthy. Captured by Parliamentary soldiers, he eventually escaped to join Charles I at Oxford. Later he fled with young Prince Charles to the Isles of Scilly. After the Restoration he returned to Luccombe, where he died in 1669. The churchyard cross was reduced to a stump during the Civil War.

DUNSTER CASTLE

Recorded as Torre in the Domesday Book, later becoming Dunestorre and eventually Dunster, there was a fortress on the steep, wooded hill overlooking the Bristol Channel in Saxon times. After the Norman Conquest the manor was given to William de Mohun, who built a castle on the 'tor' of which no trace remains. The oldest part of the present fortress is the gateway, built by Reynold de Mohun II in the first part of the thirteenth century. It adjoins the gatehouse, built in 1420 by Sir Hugh Luttrell, whose mother, Elizabeth, Lady Luttrell, bought the property from Joan, Lady de Mohun, in 1376. In the twelfth century the sea lapped the foot of the hill, but by the fifteenth, when the deer park was created, it had receded. Today the castle is about a mile inland. In 1617 George Luttrell commissioned the architect William Arnold to construct a new house, incorporating parts of the medieval building. Although its fortifications were destroyed after the Civil War, the house was spared. In 1868–72 Anthony Salvin transformed the property into the castellated and turreted mansion seen today. The Luttrells gave it to the National Trust in 1976.

TAUNTON CASTLE

Taunton, the county town of Somerset, lies in the fertile Vale of Taunton Deane, sheltered between the Quantock and Blackdown hills. Said to have been founded by Ine, King of Wessex, who built a fortress on the south bank of the River Tone in 710 (destroyed by his wife in 722), the town became an important market centre for the produce of the surrounding countryside. In Norman times the Bishops of Winchester, who owned the town, erected a stone castle on the site of the Anglo-Saxon stronghold. In 1645, during the Civil War, the castle suffered a bitter but unsuccessful siege by the Royalists in which two thirds of the town was destroyed. After the Restoration the castle was largely dismantled, together with the town's fortifications. The Great Hall, which survived, was the setting for one of Lord Chief Justice Jeffreys' infamous 'Bloody Assizes', following the Duke of Monmouth's rebellion in 1685. The building now houses the Somerset County Museum. The medieval church towers of both St Mary Magdalene and St James were rebuilt in the nineteenth century after being declared unsafe.

Photographer's Notes

QUANTOCK HILLS
from near Dowsborough

In 1798, having climbed with Coleridge to the Iron Age hillfort of Dowsborough, Dorothy Wordsworth wrote in her *Alfoxden Journal*: 'Walked to the top of a high hill to see a fortification. Again sat down to feed upon the prospect; a magnificent scene, *curiously* spread out for even minute inspection, though so extensive that the mind is afraid to calculate its bounds.' During the closing years of the eighteenth century the Wordsworths and Coleridge often explored the Quantocks. William and Dorothy lived at Alfoxton, near Holford, from July 1797 to June 1798, while from late December 1796 until Christmas 1799 Coleridge rented a dilapidated thatched cottage in Lime Street, Nether Stowey, which he occupied with his wife Sara, baby son Hartley and innumerable guests. 'My walks . . . were almost daily on the top of Quantock, and among its sloping coombs', he wrote. 'With my pencil and memorandum book in my hand, I was *making studies*, as the artists call them, and often moulding my thoughts into verse, with the objects and imagery immediately before my senses.' Coleridge Cottage, was acquired by the National Trust in 1909.

After much deliberation about the pictures for this new book, I decided to make a start at Land's End. My maps told me that this had a certain logic: travelling to the furthest point first I would then slowly work my way home, each trip involving less distance. Two weeks after I arrived, however, I still hadn't taken a single picture. A sea mist had rolled in and resolutely refused to move. It was so thick that even research was impossible. The foghorns droned on through day and night. The locals started to talk of global warming and changing weather patterns and I found myself beginning to agree. Fortunately, I had the company of my ever-faithful border collie, George, who, as always, kept me thoroughly entertained. He courted the friendship of some piglets at a smallholding at Land's End, right by the coastal footpath, and as this track lay on the course of our daily walk the friendship grew, with three piglets regularly escaping to chase George at high speed around the clifftops. I suppose I should have guessed then that this was going to be no ordinary project.

The West Country offered a fantastic choice of pictures and ever-changing conditions in which to take them. Such was the variety that I could still be there now, taking new pictures or old ones under a different light. Dartmoor, Bodmin Moor, Exmoor, Penwith or the South Hams could become a lifetime passion for me.

During this project a major back problem forced me to review the type of equipment that I used. Weight became more important than features, comfort more important than format. Strangely, as a consequence, picture-taking became more pleasurable. The equipment I used for this book consisted of two systems: a Nikon 35mm system with F3 body, years old but still working well, and 24mm, 28mm, 35mm, 85mm and 180mm lenses; a medium-format system consisting of a Mamiya 6 body and 50mm, 75mm and 150mm lenses. Each system was carried in a standard rucksack rather than a camera bag, in most cases with a tripod. I would simply choose the system most suitable for the type of picture I hoped to take. The film was Fuji Velvia, quite the sharpest and most colourful transparency stock I know of.

Rob Talbot

Selected Properties and Regional Offices

ENGLISH HERITAGE

All English Heritage properties, except where specified, are open from April to end September every day from 10am to 6pm (summer season) and from October to March, Tuesdays to Sundays, from 10am to 4pm, and are closed on 24, 25 and 26 December and 1 January.

Head Office
Keysign House
429 Oxford Street
London W1R 2HD
Tel: (071) 973 3000

South-West Regional Information Office
7–8 King Street
Bristol BS1 4EQ
Tel: (0272) 750 700

Berry Pomeroy Castle
Totnes
Devon TQ9 6NJ
Tel: (0803) 866618
Open: summer season.

Cleeve Abbey
Washford
Watchet
Somerset TA23 0PS
Tel: (0984) 40377

Dartmouth Castle
Castle Road
Dartmouth
Devon TQ6 0JN
Tel: (0803) 833588

Launceston Castle
Launceston
Cornwall PL15 7DR
Tel: (0566) 772365

Okehampton Castle
Okehampton
Devon EX20 1JB
Tel: (0837) 52844

Pendennis Castle
Falmouth
Cornwall TR11 4LP
Tel: (0326) 316594

Restormel Castle
Lostwithiel
Cornwall PL22 0DB
Tel: (0208) 872687
Open: summer season.

St Mawes Castle
St Mawes
Cornwall TR2 3AA
Tel: (0326) 270526

Tintagel Castle
Tintagel
Cornwall PL34 0AA
Tel: (0840) 770328

Totnes Castle
Totnes
Devon TQ9 5NE
Tel: (0803) 864406

NATIONAL TRUST

Cornwall Regional Office
Lanhydrock
Bodmin
Cornwall PL30 4DE
Tel: (0208) 74281

Devon Regional Office
Killerton House
Broadclyst
Exeter
Devon EX5 3LE
Tel: (0392) 881691

Wessex Regional Office
Eastleigh Court
Bishopstrow
Warminster
Wiltshire BA12 9HW
Tel: (0985) 847777

A La Ronde
Exmouth
Devon EX8 5BD
Tel: (0395) 265514
Open: April to end October, Sundays to Thursdays.

Arlington Court
Arlington
near Barnstaple
Devon EX31 4LP
Tel: (0271) 850296
Open: April to end October, Sundays to Fridays and Bank Holiday weekends.

Barrington Court
near Ilminster
Somerset TA19 0NQ
Tel: (0460) 41938
Open: April to end October; house Wednesdays only; garden Sundays to Thursdays.

Buckland Abbey
Yelverton
Devon PL20 6EY
Tel: (0822) 853607
Open: April to end October, Fridays to Wednesdays; November to March, Saturdays and Sundays.

Castle Drogo
Drewsteignton
Devon EX6 6PB
Tel: (0647) 433306
Open: April to end October; castle Saturdays to Thursdays; garden daily.

Coleridge Cottage
35 Lime Street
Nether Stowey
Bridgwater
Somerset TA5 1NQ
Tel: (0278) 732662
Open: April to end September, Tuesdays to Thursdays and Sundays.

Compton Castle
Marldon
Paignton
Devon TQ3 1TA
Tel: (0803) 872112
Open: April to end October, Mondays, Wednesdays and Thursdays.

Cotehele
St Dominick
near Saltash
Cornwall PL12 6TA
Tel: (0579) 50434
 (information) (0579) 51222
Open: April to end October; house Saturdays to Thursdays; garden daily.

Dunster Castle
Dunster
near Minehead
Somerset TA24 6SL
Tel: (0643) 821314
Open: castle April to October, Saturdays to Wednesdays; garden and park February to mid-December daily.

Glendurgan Garden
Mawnan Smith
near Falmouth
Cornwall TR11 5JZ
Tel: (0326) 250906 (opening hours only)
Open: March to end October, Tuesdays
to Saturdays and Bank Holiday Mondays
(closed: Good Friday).

Lanhydrock House
Bodmin
Cornwall PL30 5AD
Tel: (0208) 73320
Open: April to end October, house
Tuesdays to Sundays and Bank Holiday
Mondays; garden daily.

Lydford Gorge
The Stables
Lydford Gorge
Lydford
near Okehampton
Devon EX20 4BH
Tel: (082 282) 441/320
Open: daily throughout the year, but
limited access November to March.

Overbeck's Museum & Garden
Sharpitor
Salcombe
Devon TQ8 8LW
Tel: (054 884) 2893
Open: museum April to end October,
Sundays to Fridays; garden daily
throughout the year.

St Michael's Mount
Marazion
near Penzance
Cornwall TR17 0HT
Tel: (0736) 710507
Open: April to end October, Mondays to
Fridays and some weekends; November
to March limited access.

Tintagel Old Post Office
Tintagel
Cornwall PL34 0DB
Tel: (0840) 770024 (opening hours only)
Open: April to end October, daily.

Trelissick Garden
Feock
near Truro
Cornwall TR3 6QL
Tel: (0872) 862090
    or (0872) 865808 (information)
Open: March to end October, daily.

Trengwainton Garden
near Penzance
Cornwall TR20 8RZ
Tel: (0736) 63021
Open: March to end October,
Wednesdays to
Saturdays and Bank Holiday Mondays.

Trerice
near Newquay
Cornwall TR8 4PG
Tel: (0637) 875404
Open: April to end October, Wednesdays
to Mondays.

Watersmeet House
Watersmeet Road
Lynmouth
Devon EX35 6NT
Tel: (0598) 53348
Open: April to end October, daily.

NATIONAL PARKS

Dartmoor National Park Authority
Parke
Haytor Road
Bovey Tracey
Devon TQ13 9JQ
Tel: (0626) 832093

Exmoor National Park Authority
Exmoor House
Dulverton
Somerset TA22 9HL
Tel: (0398) 23665

MISCELLANEOUS

Bickleigh Castle
Bickleigh
near Tiverton
Devon EX16 8RP
Tel: (0884) 855363
Open: end May Bank Holiday to early

October, Sundays to Fridays; Easter to
end May, Wednesdays, Sundays and
Bank Holidays.

Buckfast Abbey
Buckfastleigh
Devon TQ11 0EE
Tel: (0362) 42519
Open: daily throughout the year.

Canonteign Falls and Country Park
Lower Ashton
near Chudleigh
Devon EX6 7RH
Tel: (0647) 52434
Open: Easter to end October, daily;
winter, Sundays and school holidays.

Devonshire's Centre
Bickleigh
near Tiverton
Devon EX16 8RG
Tel: (0884) 855419
Open: Easter to Christmas, daily; January
to March, Saturdays and Sundays.

Gwennap Pit
Busveal
Redruth
Cornwall
Open: daily throughout the year.

Hartland Abbey
near Bideford
Devon EX39 6DT
Tel: (0237) 441264
Open: May to September, Wednesdays
and Bank Holiday Mondays; July to
mid-September, Wednesdays and
Sundays.

Kent's Cavern
Torquay
Devon TQ1 2JF
Tel: (0803) 294059
Open: daily throughout the year.

The Minack Theatre
Porthcurno
Penzance
Cornwall TR19 6JU
Tel: (office) (0736) 810694
    (bookings) (0736) 810471
Performances: end May to
mid-September, Mondays to Fridays.
Exhibition Centre: end March to end
October, daily.

Oldway Mansion
Paignton
Devon
Tel: (0803) 296244
Open: daily, except Saturday and Sunday
afternoons during winter.

Poldark Mine & Heritage Complex
Helston
Cornwall TR13 0ER
Tel: (0326) 573173
Open: end March to end October, daily.

Waterfall and Hermitage
St Nectan's Glen
Tintagel
Cornwall PL34 0BE
Tel: (0840) 770760
Open: daily throughout the year.

Wheal Martyn Museum
Carthew
St Austell
Cornwall PL26 8XG
Tel: (0726) 850362
Open: Easter to end October, daily.

Select Bibliography

Ashe, Geoffrey, *The Landscape of King Arthur*, Webb & Bower, Exeter, 1987

Baker, C. Jane (intro.), *A Vision of Dartmoor*, Gollancz, London, 1988

Baring-Gould, S., *The Vicar of Morwenstow*, Methuen, London, 1899

Barton, D. B., *A History of Copper Mining in Cornwall and Devon*, Bradford Barton, Truro, 1961

   A History of Tin Mining and Smelting in Cornwall, Bradford Barton, Truro, 1965 (rev. 1969)

Bird, Sheila, *The Book of Cornish Villages*, Dovecote Press, Wimborne, 1988

   Cornish Curiosities, Dovecote Press, Wimborne, 1989

Borlase, William, *Cornish Antiquities*, 1754

Carew, Richard, *The Survey of Cornwall*, 1602 (New Edition, London, 1769)

Carrington, Nicholas Toms, *Dartmoor: a Descriptive Poem*, John Murray, London, 1826

Cohen, J. M., (ed.) *The Itinerary of John Leland: Vol. I*, Southern University Press, Carbondale, USA, 1964

Court, Glyn, *Exmoor National Park*, Webb and Bower, Exeter, 1987

Cox, Thomas, *Magna Britannia et Hibernia: Devonshire*, 1720

Coxe, Antony D. Hippisley, *Smuggling in the West Country 1700–1850*, Tabb House, Padstow, 1984

Crossing, William, *The Ancient Stone Crosses of Dartmoor*, Devon books, Exeter, 1987

   Guide to Dartmoor: A Topographical Description of the Forest and Commons, 1912 (reprinted David and Charles, 1965)

Dartmoor: National Park Guide No 1, HMSO, 1957 (rep. 1979)

Deane, Tony, and Shaw, Tony, *The Folklore of Cornwall*, Batsford, London, 1975

Du Maurier, Daphne, *Enchanted Cornwall*, Michael Joseph, Harmondsworth, 1989

   Vanishing Cornwall: The Spirit & History of Cornwall, Gollancz, London, 1967

Durrance, E. M. and Laming, D. J. C. (eds), *The Geology of Devon*, University of Exeter, 1982

Egeland, Pamela, *Cob and Thatch*, Devon Books, Exeter, 1988

Fox, Aileen, *South-West England: 3,500 BC–AD 600*, David & Charles, Newton Abbot, 1964

Gill, Crispin, (ed.), *Dartmoor: A New Study*, David & Charles, Newton Abbot, 1970

Gill, Crispin, *The Duchy of Cornwall*, David & Charles, Newton Abbot, 1987

Harris, Helen, *Industrial Archaeology of Dartmoor*, David & Charles, Newton Abbot, 1968

Jenkin, A. K. Hamilton, *Cornwall and its People*, Dent, London, 1945

   The Story of Cornwall, Nelson, London, 1934

John, Catherine Rachel, *The Saints of Cornwall*, Dyllansow Truran, Redruth, 1981

Laws, Peter, *A Guide to the National Trust in Devon and Cornwall*, David & Charles, Newton Abbot, 1978

Little, Roger Irving, (comp.) *Boscastle*, Camelot Pottery, Boscastle, 1970

Maber, Richard, and Tregoning, Angela, (eds) *Kilvert's Cornish Diary*, Alison Hodge, Penzance, 1989

Mayberry, Tom, *Coleridge & Wordsworth in the West Country*, Alan Sutton, Stroud, 1992

Mee, Arthur, *Devon* (King's England series), Hodder and Stoughton, London, 1938

Minchinton, Walter, *Devon's Industrial Past: a Guide*, Dartington Centre for Education & Research, Dartington, 1986

Murray's Handbook for Devon & Cornwall (1859), rep. David & Charles, Newton Abbot, 1971

Nix, Michael, and Myers, Mark R., *Hartland Quay: the Story of a Vanished Port*, Hartland Quay Museum, Hartland, 1982

Northcote, Lady Rosalind, *Devon*, Chatto & Windus, London, 1919

Nowakowski, Jacqueline A., and Thomas, Charles, *Excavations at Tintagel Parish Churchyard Cornwall, Spring 1990 (Interim Report)*, Cornwall Archaeological Unit & Institute of Cornish Studies, Truro, 1990

Palmer, Kingsley, *The Folklore of Somerset*, Batsford, London, 1976

Pevsner, Nikolaus, *South and West Somerset* (Buildings of England series), Penguin, Harmondsworth, 1958

Pevsner, Nikolaus, and Cherry, Bridget, *Devon* (Buildings of England series), Penguin, Harmondsworth, 1952 (rev. 1989)

Pevsner, Nikolaus, and Radcliffe, Enid, *Cornwall* (Buildings of England series), Penguin, Harmondsworth, 1970

Ravensdale, Jack, *National Trust Histories: Cornwall*, Willow, London, 1984

Salmon, Arthur L., (rev. Hicks, H. Ronald), *The Little Guide: Cornwall*, Methuen, London, 1903

Saunders, Andrew, *Exploring Britain's Heritage: Devon and Cornwall*, HMSO, London, 1991

Starkey, F. H., *Dartmoor Crosses & Some Ancient Tracks*, Starkey, 1983 (rev. 1989)

Steers, J. A., *The Coastline of England and Wales*, University Press, Cambridge, 1969

Taylor, John, *Wandering to See the Wonders of the West (1649)*, Graham, Newcastle upon Tyne, facs. of 1873, pub. 1967

Thorpe, Lewis, (trans.), *Geoffrey of Monmouth: The History of the Kings of Britain*, Folio Society, London, 1969

Wace and Layamon, *Arthurian Chronicles*, (intro. Gwyn Jones), Dent, London, 1962

Weatherhill, Craig, *Belerion: Ancient Sites of Land's End*, Alison Hodge, Penzance, 1981

   Cornovia: Ancient Sites of Cornwall & Scilly, Alison Hodge, Penzance, 1985

Weir, John, *Dartmoor National Park*, Webb & Bower, London, 1987

Whitlock, Ralph, *The Folklore of Devon*, Batsford, London, 1977

Index

Page numbers in *italics* denote photographs.

Acland, Sir Thomas Dyke, 58, 147, 149, 150
A La Ronde, *120*
Alfred the Great, King, 93, 132
Allerford, *150*
Altarnun, 67
Appledore, 132, *133*
Arlington Court, *132*
Arthur, King, 10, 28, 55–7, 60, 63, 70
Ashburton, 35, 96, 99, 104, 107
Athelstan, King of Wessex, 48, 74, 115

Baggy Point, 130
Barnstaple, 129, 132
Bedruthan Steps, *36*, 37
Beer, 115, 124, 126
Bennet's Cross, *102*, 103
Berry Pomeroy Castle, *90*, 91
Betjeman, Sir John, 65, 139
Bickleigh, 126, *127*
Bideford, 129, 135
Bigbury Bay, 80, *81*
Bodmin, 69, 137
Bodmin Moor, 14, 28, 33, 35, 50, 60, 67, 70, 73
    115, 155
Boscastle, *54*, 55, 63, 138
Bossington, 149
Bottalack Mine, 20, *21*
Bovey Tracey, 99
Bowerman's Nose, *8*, 9, 100
Branscombe, 124
Brentor, *110*, 111
Brixham, 86, *87*, 139
Brown Willy, 67
Buckfast Abbey, *96*
Buckfastleigh, 100
Buckland Abbey, *76*, 77, 115
Buckland-in-the-Moor, 99
Bude, 58, *59*
Bull Point Lighthouse, *130*
Burgh Island, 80, *81*

Cadgwith Cove, 28, *29*
Cambourne, 26, 41
Camelford, 56, 57, 67, 116
Canonteign Falls and Country Park, 97
Cape Cornwall, 22

Carn Brea Castle, 14, *40*, 41
Carn Euny Iron Age Settlement, 10
Carnmenellis, 33, 115
Carrick Roads, 43, 44, 47
Castle-an-Dinas, 10
Castle Dore, 50
Castle Drogo, *113*
Castlesteads, 57
Cawsand, 74
Chagford, 35, 103, 104, 113
Chambercombe Manor, 129
Chapel Rock, *38*, 39
Charles I, King, 9, 43, 150
Charles II, King, 26, 43, 44, 150
Cheesewring, 70
Christie, Agatha, 80, 88, 138
Chudleigh, 97
Chun Castle, 13, 20
Chysauster Ancient Village, 10, *11*, 15
Clovelly, *135*, 137
Cockington, *91*
Coleridge, Samuel Taylor, 123, 137, 140, 145, 155
Combe Martin, 132
Come-to-Good Meeting House, *44*
Compass Point, 58, *59*
Cornworthy, 116
Cranmere Pool, 113
Crantock Beach, 37
Crediton, 74, 115
Crockern Tor, 103, 104
Croyde, 130, *131*
Culbone, 137, *144*, 145, 147
Cullompton, *126*
Culmstock, 137

Dart, River, 86, 96, 99, 138
Dartmoor, 9–10, 14, 33, 60, 93–4, 100, 103, 104,
    107, 109, 111, 113, 115, 119, 137, 142, 155
Dartmouth, 86, 139
Dartmouth Castle, *86*, 116
Davy, Humphrey, 26
Dawlish, *119*
Dawlish Warren, 120
Daymer Bay, 14
Delabole, 55, 65, 67, 116
Devonport Dockyard, 77, 84

Downsborough, 155
Doyden Point, *64*, 65
Dozmary Pool, 28, 48, 57, *70*
Drake, Sir Francis, 77–8, 86, 93
Drewsteignton, 113
Droskyn Point, *38*, 39
Dulverton, 145
Du Maurier, Daphne, 67, 138
Dunkery Beacon, 9, 150
Dunster Castle, *152*, 153

Eddystone Lighthouse, 74, 78
Edward I, King, 33, 147
Edward III, King, 60
Edward VI, King, 91
Edward the Black Prince, 53, 60, 94
Edward the Confessor, King, 26, 91
Elizabeth I, Queen, 37, 77–8
Exe, River, 115, 120, 126, 145
Exeter, 74, 88, 99, 115, 119, 126, 138, 147
Exeter Cathedral, *114*, 115, 123, 124
Exmoor, 9, 93, 115, 120, 137, 140, 142, 147, 150,
    155
Exmouth, 120, *121*

Falmouth, 30, 34, *42*, 43, 44, 47
Fernworthy, 103
Fowey, 50, *51*, 138
Fowey, River, 50, *51*, 53, 67, 69
Frobisher, Sir Martin, 78

Gannel, River, 37
Gilbert, Sir Humphrey, 78, 138
Godrevy Lighthouse, *16*
Goonhilly Satellite Earth Station, 30
Grenville, Sir Richard, 55, 77–8
Grey Wethers Stone Circles, *103*
Grimspound, 100, *101*
Gumb, Daniel, 70
Gunwalloe, 28
Gwennap Pit, *41*

Hallsands, 83, *84*
Hardy, Thomas, 9, 138
Hartland, 63, 139
Hartland Point Lighthouse, *134*, 135

Hawker, R. S., 58, 138
Hawkins, Sir Christopher, 48
Hawkins, Sir John, 77–8
Hawkridge, 147
Hayes Barton, 78
Haytor, 100
Helston, 10, 28, 33, 35
Henry I, King, 60, 93
Henry VI, King, 26
Henry VIII, King, 43, 47, 50, 83, 91, 103, 111,
    123
Hensbarrow Downs, 33, 35, 48, 115
High Peak, 120, *121*
Holne, 99, 137
Holnicote Estate, 149, 150
Holsworthy, 58
Hooken Cliffs, *124*
Hookney Tor, 100
Hound Tor, *100*
Hurlers, The, *72*, 73

Ilfracombe, *128*, 129, 132, 135
Ine, King of Wessex, 153
Instow, 132

Jamaica Inn, 67, 138
James II, King, 86
John, King, 33, 93

Kent's Cavern, 13
Killigrew, Sir John, 30, 43
King Doniert's Stone, 69
Kingsand, 74
Kingsbridge, 83
Kingsley, Charles, 99, 132, 137
Kingswear Castle, 86
Kirkham House, 88

Landacre Bridge, *146*, 147
Land's End, 13–14, 22, *23*, 33, 35, 115, 155
Lanhydrock House, *68*, 69
Lanyon Quoit, *12*, 13
Launceston, 58, 109, 116
Lawrence, D. H., 19, 138
Levant Mine, 20
Lew Trenchard, 138

Linkinhorne, 70
Liskeard, 33, 73, 74
Lizard, The, 28, 30, *31*, 115
Loe Bar and Pool, *28*, 57
Logan Rock, 24
Lostwithiel, 33, 50, 53
Luccombe, 149, 150, *151*
Lundy Island, 129, 135
Lydford, 93–4, 109
Lydford Castle, 93–4, *95*
Lydford Gorge, *109*
Lynmouth, 137, 140, *141*, 142
Lynton, 140

Madron, 13, 20
Maenporth, 14
Manaton, 9, 100
Marazion, 26
Marconi, Guglielmo, 30
Mary Tavy, 109
Menacuddle Baptistry, *52*, 53
Men-an-Tol, *20*
Men Scryfa, 20
Merlin's Cave, *62*, 63
Merrivale Stone Rows, *106*, 107
Mevagissey, *50*, 115
Minack Theatre, *24*
Minehead, 124
Minions, 39
Moretonhampstead, 103, 104
Morte Point, 130
Morvah, 20
Morwenstow, *58*, 138
Mount Edgcumbe Country Park, 74
Mount's Bay, 14
Mousehole, 24, *25*, 26
Mullion Cove, *30*
Murdoch, William, 41

Nether Stowey, 137, 155
Newcomen, Thomas, 35, 86
Newlyn, 24, *26*
Newton Abbot, 115, 119
Newton Ferrers, 80
Newquay, 37, 39
Nine Maidens Stone Circle, 20
Northam, 132
Northernhay, 115
Noss Mayo, *80*

Oare, *136*, 137, 147
Oare Common, 142, *143*
Okehampton Castle, *111*
Oldway Mansion, 88, *89*

Opie, John, 39
Otter, River, 116, 123
Otterton, 116, *117*
Ottery St Mary, 123, 137
Overbeck Museum, 83

Padstow, 56, 115, 138
Paignton, 86, 88, 91
Pendennis Castle, *43*, 47
Pendour Cove, 19
Pendower Beach, 14
Penlee, 24
Penlee Point, 74
Penpol, 44
Penryn, 43
Pentire Point, 65
Penwith, 26, 35, 155
Penzance, 10, 24, *26*
Perranporth, 39
Pilgrim Fathers, 78
Plymouth, 74, 77, 84, 86, 104, 109, 115, 119
Plymouth Hoe, 77, 78, *79*
Plymouth Sound, 74, 77, 78, 111
Plympton, 35, 104
Poldhu, 30
Polpeor Cove, *1*
Polperro, *2*
Poltesco, 28
Polzeath, 139
Porlock, 137, 145, 147, 149, 150
Porlock, Vale of, *148*, 149
Port Eliot, 74
Port Gaverne, 65
Porthcurno, 24
Porthleven, 28
Porthmeor, 15
Port Isaac, 65, *66*, 67
Portquin, 65
Postbridge, 103, *104*
Princetown, 94, 104
Probus, *48*
Prussia Cove, 129

Quantock Hills, 137, 140, 153, *154*, 155
Quiller-Couch, Sir Arthur, 50, 137–38

Raleigh, Sir Walter, *43*, 77, 78, 120
Rame Head, 74, 75
Redruth, 14, 33, 35, 41
Restormel Castle, *53*
Revelstoke, 80
Rillaton Barrow, 73
Roche Rock, 48, *49*
Rock, 65

Rocky Valley, *60*
Roseland Peninsula, 44, 47
Rougemont Castle, 115

St Agnes, 33, 35, *39*
St Austell, 33, 35, 50, 53, 138
St Catherine's Castle, 50
St Cleer, 69
St Enodoc's Church, *65*, 139
St Germanus' Church, *74*
St Ives, 16, *17*, 19
St Juliot, 138
St Just, 20, 22
St Just in Roseland, 44, *45*
St Mawes, 44, *46*, 47
St Mawes Castle, *43*, 47
St Michael's Mount, 15, 26, *27*, 30
St Minver, 65
St Nectan's Glen, 60, *63*
Salcombe, *82*, 83
Scilly, Isles of, 13, 14, 22, 26, 150
Scorhill Circle, *112*, 113
Selworthy, *149*, 150
Sharpitor, 83
Sid, River, 123
Sidmouth, *122*, 123
Simonsbath, 145, 147
Slapton Ley, 83, 84, *85*
Slaughter Bridge, 56, 57
South-West Coast Path, 19, 65, 124
Starcross, 119
Start Point, *83*
Stephen, King, 96
Stoke Bay, 80
Stoke Pero, *147*
Stowe's Hill, 70, *71*
Strete-Undercliffe, 83

Tamar, River, 77, 109
Tarr Steps, *145*
Taunton, 137, 153
Taunton Castle, *153*
Tavistock, 35, 77, *92*, 93, 104, 107, 116
Tavy, River, 93
Taw, River, 132
Teign, River, 113, 119
Teignmouth, *118*, 119
Temple, 67
Tennyson, Alfred, 57, 77
Tintagel, 55, 56, 63
Tintagel Castle, 55, 57, 60, *61*, 63
Tiverton, 120, 126, 137
Tolmen Stone, 113
Topsham, 120

Torcross, 84
Torre Abbey, 88
Torridge, River, 132, 139
Torquay, 13, 86, *88*, 91, 115, 138
Totnes, 86, 91, 116
Towanroath Engine House, *32*, 33
Trebetherick, 65, 139
Tregerthen, *19*
Tremedda, *19*
Trethevy Quoit, *73*
Trethowel, 53
Trevaunance Porth, 39
Trevellas, 39
Trevithick, Richard, 35, 41
Trevowhan, 13, 20
Trewithen, 48
Tristan Stone, 50
Truro, 33, *34*, 35, 39, 44, 47, 69, 74
Two Bridges, 104
Two Moors Way, 145

Valley of the Rocks, *140*
Veryan, *47*
Victoria, Queen, 34, 123

Wadebridge, 56, 67
Warren House Inn, 103, 104
Watersmeet, *142*
Watt, James, 35
Westward Ho!, 132, 137
Wheal Betsy Mine, *108*, 109
Wheal Coates Mine, 33
Wheal Friendship Mine, 109
Whitsand Bay, 74
Widecombe-in-the-Moor, 94, *98*, 99
William I, King, 115
William, Prince of Orange, 86
Wimbleball Lake, 142
Wimborne, 57
Winsford Hill, 142
Wistman's Wood, 104, *105*
Withypool, 145, 147
Withypool Common, 142
Woolf, Virginia, 16, 138
Wootton Courtenay, 149
Wordsworth, William and Dorothy, 137, 155

Yealm, River, 80
Yenworthy Common, 142

Zennor, 16, *18*, 19, 138